THE ESSENTIAL MAGGIE McNEILL

VOLUME I

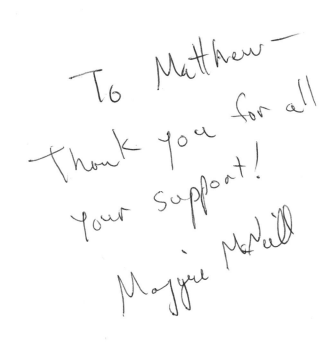

To Matthew —
Thank you for all
your support!
Maggie McNeill

THE ESSENTIAL

MAGGIE McNEILL

VOLUME I

Collected essays from *The Honest Courtesan*

---------------First Edition, January 2020---------------

All of the essays within previously appeared in *The Honest Courtesan* (http://maggiemcneill.wordpress.com/) on the following dates: "Creating Criminals" (January 15th, 2011); "Skin To Skin" (February 17th, 2013); "Godwin's Law" (March 5th, 2011); "A Necessary Evil" (April 25th, 2012); "The Daughters of Shamhat" (May 24th, 2012); "The Birth of a Movement" (June 2nd, 2012); "The Fourth of July" (July 4th, 2012); "Advice for Clients" (August 21st, 2010); "Enough is Enough" (September 5th, 2012); "Heart of Gold" (October 6th, 2010); "The Source" (November 27th, 2012); "Ignoble Experiment" (December 5th, 2013); "Not for Everybody" (January 17th, 2012); "Straining at Gnats" (February 24th, 2013); "Circle" (March 14th, 2012); "The Rape Question" (April 4th, 2012); "Heroines" (May 16th, 2011); "Dirty Whores" (June 24th, 2011); "Bogeymen" (July 27th, 2012); "The Privilege Paradigm" (August 22nd, 2013); "Against Conscience" (September 12th, 2012); "The Love-Hate Relationship" (October 7th, 2010); "The Dance of Death" (November 1st, 2013); "Thought Experiment" (December 16th, 2011); "Objectification Overruled" (January 31st, 2012); "The Pygmalion Fallacy" (May 6th, 2012); "Vulnerability" (March 8th, 2013); "The Suppression of Virtue" (June 14th, 2012); "Chauvinism" (May 3rd, 2013); "Don't Try This At Home" (June 23rd, 2014); "Cleaning Toilets" (July 25th, 2013); "Ulro" (August 12th, 2016); "The Girls from Tarzana" (September 12th, 2011); "Amazingly Stupid Statements" (October 10th, 2010); "Honored in the Breach" (November 6th, 2012); "Like a Horse and Carriage" (December 10th, 2012); "Somebody's Daughter" (September 11th, 2012); "A False Dichotomy" (June 22nd, 2011); "Harlots of the Bible" (July 22nd, 2011); "Imagination Pinned Down" (June 12th, 2012); "The Kisaeng" (September 12th, 2013); "Magic Formulae" (June 20th, 2013); "An Older Profession Than You May Have Thought" (October 12th, 2010); "The Pit" (January 2nd, 2014); "Quite Contrary" (June 8th, 2012); "Rooted in Racism" (June 29th, 2011); "Tales from the Dark Side" (May 9th, 2013); "Universal Criminality" (January 15th, 2012); "Whorearchy" (May 10th, 2012); "Storyville" (September 3rd, 2010); "Honolulu Harlots" (July 5th, 2011); and "Cleansing Fire" (November 5th, 2013).

First Edition, January 2020
ISBN 1-724426-05-2
Printed in the United States of America
http://maggiemcneill.wordpress.com/

For Grace, without whom it
would have been impossible

Table of Contents

The Essential Maggie McNeill

Foreword

My name is Maggie McNeill, and I'm a whore. Most of you reading this probably already know that, and many of you may already be regular readers. But for those who *didn't* know, and are shocked by my casual use of a word you might consider ugly and/or pejorative, I should probably explain that I mean it quite literally: I am a prostitute. A harlot. A lady of the night. I charge for sex, and have been doing so at least intermittently for literally my entire adult life, since January of 1985; I've been doing sex work full time since January 2000. Furthermore, I've been agitating for the decriminalization of sex work since autumn 2004, and writing my blog *The Honest Courtesan* (maggiemcneill.wordpress.com) since July 10th, 2010. In all that time I've never missed a day, which means that of this writing – on the eve of the 8th anniversary of my blog – I've now racked up almost 3000 essays. And since I've been promising my readers a "best of" collection since the beginning of 2014, I thought it was high time I delivered. I hope that those of you who were previously unfamiliar with my work like what you see and keep reading.

The 52 essays in this collection were all originally written and published on my blog between 2010 and 2016; because of that, most of them have been edited or even slightly rewritten to one degree or another. Some of that editing was to eliminate language like "yesterday I wrote such-and-such" or "this thing happened last week"; some of it was to reword references to then-current events so as to reflect their greater distance in the past; and some of it (especially in the oldest essays) was to correct wording I now see as clumsy or unnecessarily abrasive, or to bring older essays into conformation with my current style (which seems to me to have reached maturity in 2012). One thing I haven't much changed is my usage of the word "prostitute"; though I dislike the word because it's both legalistic and pejorative, there really aren't a lot of non-colloquial alternatives other than "whore" and "harlot". Obviously there's "sex worker", and sometimes I do use that; however, that term refers to *any*one who sells erotic services, including strippers, porn performers, phone sex operators, dominatrices, etc, and sometimes (especially when discussing laws) I want to specify that kind of sex work which usually includes the direct and hands-on provision of an orgasm. So I'm kind of stuck with an ugly word until someone comes up with a better one which is just as precise.

Not all of the essays herein are about sex work; many are about government tyranny, some are philosophical, and a few are on popular culture and similar topics. They represent half of what I consider my best work from the covered time period; the other half will be in the forthcoming volume II. Regular readers may note that neither of the volumes contain examples of my popular agony aunt columns (which will appear in a forthcoming two-volume set named *Ask Maggie*), nor any biographies of famous whores (which will appear in a volume called *Harlotography*); essays from later than 2016 will appear in a third volume of the current series, probably sometime next year. If you're a regular reader, I hope this collection makes it easier for you to share my work with others; if you're a new reader, there's more to come (and you may also enjoy my two short story collections). But in any case, I hope these essays will give you food for thought and maybe even teach you a thing or two.

Creating Criminals

**There's no way to rule innocent men. The only power
any government has is the power to crack down on
criminals. Well, when there aren't enough criminals one
makes them. One declares so many things to be a crime
that it becomes impossible for men to live without
breaking laws. Who wants a nation of law-abiding
citizens? What's there in that for anyone? But just pass
the kind of laws that can neither be observed nor
enforced or objectively interpreted – and you create a
nation of law-breakers – and then you cash in on guilt. –**
Ayn Rand, *Atlas Shrugged*

The word "lawhead" is my own coinage; it refers to
one who believes that man-made laws are actually based in
objective reality like physical laws. The lawhead is unable to
comprehend that the majority of laws are completely
arbitrary, and therefore views a violation of a "vice law" with
the same horror that normal people reserve for rains of toads
or spontaneous human combustion. Though lawheads are a
minority of the population they are disproportionately
represented in positions of power, with the result that once a
law is on the books it cannot usually be removed by any
means short of armed insurrection. Lawheads are most
dangerous when they work in close association with control
freaks, those who know very well that laws are arbitrary but
enact them anyway so as to have more excuses to threaten,
intimidate, arrest, fine and imprison the citizenry.

Most laws are usually designed with sufficiently
diabolical cleverness so as to fool the Great Unwashed into
thinking they do indeed have a basis in reality, especially

5

when enacted in conjunction with a moral panic (such as "national security", "child welfare" or the like). But even when they aren't, there are sufficient numbers of lawheads around to ensure that these tyrannical laws are rarely, if ever removed. And even when they are, for every repressive statute which is struck down ten more have been enacted in the meantime. Governments don't care *how* universal criminality (*see page 188*) is achieved, so long as it is; if it isn't done by prohibiting drinking it will be by banning smoking, and if not by forbidding homosexuality and abortion it'll be by denying privacy and the right to self-defense. And as we're seeing in many places, control freaks are equally happy demonizing our clients as they ever were demonizing whores. The important thing is to define as many people as possible as criminals, thereby inducing a kind of social autoimmune disorder for which government can be touted as the cure though it is actually the cause.

Take the Jim Crow laws, for example, which were designed to control free black people in the latter half of the 19th century; all manner of things were made illegal for them so that governments would have the excuse to monitor, harass and persecute them. But after the successes of the civil rights movement in the middle of the 20th century, government somehow succeeded in casting itself as the great savior of black Americans even though it was government which had created the laws which criminalized them in the first place. The Jim Crow laws were a clumsy attempt at control because they directly targeted one obvious segment of the population. They thus A) did not intimidate everyone; and B) disallowed those in the targeted group any illusion of escape through "correct" behavior. By comparison, the anti-prostitution laws which proliferated a generation after the first Jim Crow laws affected almost 10% of women and 70%

of men and were thus far more effective means of social control; a few years later alcohol prohibition was still *more* efficient at creating criminals out of previously law-abiding citizens.

At the stroke of a pen, the 18th Amendment magically transformed tens of millions of ordinary Americans, no different from their neighbors, into criminals, and many millions of others lost respect for all law and authority due to the rigor with which the asinine prohibition law was enforced. Deprived of legal sources of alcohol, Americans turned to those who could supply it, thus enriching true criminals (gangsters and smugglers), and enticing many who might not otherwise ever have crossed the line into the now-lucrative bootlegging market. Tens of thousands were blinded, paralyzed, and killed by moonshine made from industrial alcohol the government had intentionally poisoned to keep people from drinking it (*see page 49*). Official corruption ran rampant, courts and prisons were clogged with people who had not been considered criminals a few years earlier, federal police powers were dangerously expanded, and civil liberties were bulldozed in order to enforce a law which was unjust and unenforceable to begin with, and billions were wasted on enforcement while billions more were lost in tax revenues.

This was, of course, utterly incomprehensible to lawheads; those who made statements on the subject in 1920 predicted that the law would magically remove the desire for liquor from the American mind. The Internal Revenue Service predicted that the law would be instantly effective, but that it would take six years for all existing private liquor supplies to be used up. And Prohibitionists both inside and

7

outside the government questioned neither the ability to legislate state-defined morality into existence nor the rectitude of attempting to do so. Unfortunately, the fact that the so-called "Noble Experiment" failed miserably in less than a decade (calls for its repeal were widespread and vocal by 1929) did absolutely nothing to penetrate the thick skulls of lawheads and control freaks, who have in the intervening 80-plus years continued to support other prohibitionist bans and even foisted upon us a host of new ones.

Each of these bans – from marijuana to prostitution to pseudoephedrine – have had exactly the same effects: None of them have affected demand one iota, nor hampered those who wish to partake. All of them have enriched criminals and increased true crime and bloodshed. All of them have enticed millions who might not otherwise have committed crimes into participating in the lucrative black markets created by their prohibition. All have increased the danger to users or sellers of the banned product or service (and even to innocent bystanders), often to fatal levels. All have given rise to rampant corruption, overwhelmed court and prison systems, dangerously expanded governmental powers, and negated civil liberties; all have caused the waste of billions on enforcement and the loss of billions more in tax revenues. And each has admirably accomplished what it was enacted to accomplish: the redefinition of large segments of the population from citizens to criminals, thus allowing government yet another excuse to deprive them of their rights, goods and freedoms.

Skin To Skin

Few people would deny the importance of skin-to-skin contact in the psychological, emotional and even physical health of the newborn infant; study after study since Harlow's seminal work with Rhesus monkeys in the 1950s have demonstrated that even if all of a baby's physical needs are met clinically and dispassionately, it will not thrive in the same way as one whose bare flesh is pressed against that of its mother. Indeed, in some cases an infant deprived of this contact will actually sicken and lose weight. As time goes on, the need becomes less critical; adults can survive without it for much longer periods than babies, and some people manage to go years without touching the naked skin of another person. But though an adult deprived of such contact is not likely to die, the effect can still be quite harmful; despite the denials of prudes and others who wish to control sexuality, physical intimacy with others is indeed a basic human need, and denying people the right to obtain it from consenting partners is a cruelty verging on barbarism.

In some countries, these statements would be wholly uncontroversial and it would be difficult to find a health professional, lay person or even politician who disagreed with them. But in others (especially the United States and United Kingdom) the idea of sex as more closely akin to food, sleep and shelter than to television watching is a politically unpopular one, and I'm never surprised to see yo-yos insisting that sex is no more vital to health than candy. I'm afraid I must politely disagree with them; even in my private life I've seen too many examples of the erratic behavior of men long deprived of sex to ignore it, and as a

9

sex worker I'm privileged to be a regular witness to the profound restorative effects of simple human touch. The power was demonstrated to me most dramatically after Hurricane Katrina, when the male population in New Orleans outnumbered the female by a substantial margin and many a client was willing to pay me just to hold and touch him gently, without anything a literal-minded person would describe as "sex".

For most healthy, socially-adept adults – especially women – the distinction is at best an academic one, because they have little or no trouble securing voluntary sex partners on a regular (or at least occasional) basis. But this is not so for everyone; some people (a highly disproportionate fraction of them male) have a great deal of trouble attracting partners willing to give them sex for the usual "socially acceptable" reasons such as love, lust, gratitude, or even pity, leaving them unable to obtain it except by purchase. And if a society criminalizes that option (or creates so many impediments to commercial sex that it might as well be illegal), even that route is closed to the man who is too afraid of the police or social censure to take the risk.

Every so often the topic of sex work and disability pops up into the public consciousness; perhaps it'll happen due to a TV documentary or the release of a movie such as *The Sessions*, or maybe someone will announce plans to open a brothel with accommodations for the disabled, or a high-profile sex worker like me will write or speak about it in a major venue. The amazing sex worker and activist Rachel Wotton founded an Australian charity called "Touching Base" which works to connect disabled clients with sex workers willing to provide for their needs, and is the subject of the documentary *Scarlet Road*; she gives talks and interviews on the subject regularly. In some countries, there are even government agencies to help the disabled with their sexual needs. As a result, I think all but the most sex-negative can be helped to recognize that disabled people have the same need for intimacy as everyone else. Unfortunately, what many people fail to understand is that not all disabilities are physical, and fewer people are sympathetic to the sexual needs of men whose disabilities are less visible.

On October 17th, 2010 I published "No Other Option", in which I described my work with men burdened with physical disabilities such as blindness, cerebral palsy, paralysis or deformity resulting from terrible accidents, and even extreme obesity. But in the months that followed that essay, the majority of men who wrote to thank me for speaking up for them suffered from "invisible" disabilities such as autism, stuttering, schizophrenia or even crippling social anxiety. Like those with problems more obvious to outside observers, they found it difficult or even impossible to interact with women in the way most men take for granted, and as a result relied on sex workers for that contact. A number of them asked my advice in finding the right sex worker for their needs, and one corresponded with me about his plans to travel to Nevada to lose his virginity in a legal brothel, and shared his joy with me afterward.

If someone were to seriously argue that it was wrong to pay for food, and that the restaurant business was by its very nature exploitative and demeaning, we would dismiss him as a crank or a lunatic; if a politician were to propose laws against the buying and selling of shelter, clothing, entertainment, medical care, or other needs, he would be ridiculed in the press and his chances for re-election would be seriously in doubt. Yet sex workers are attacked thus every day; our agency is denied, our clients and employees are demonized, our profession is ridiculed and the very real social value of our work is dismissed. And though we ourselves are the chief victims of this persecution, we should never forget that there are others as well: those people who rely upon us to provide a basic human need which, if not strictly necessary for mere biological survival, is nonetheless vital to make life worthwhile.

Godwin's Law

As an online discussion grows longer, the probability of a comparison involving Nazis or Hitler approaches 1. – Mike Godwin

Most well-informed internet users are familiar with Godwin's Law, a humorous observation which acknowledges the fact that since the Nazi regime in general and Hitler in particular are widely viewed as the very worst recent examples of human behavior imaginable, they are often invoked when a critic or debater wishes to vilify his opponent in the most extreme manner possible. Mike Godwin has written (both in articles and in his book *Cyber Rights*) that it is precisely *because* such comparisons are sometimes appropriate (as in discussions about propaganda, eugenics or oppressive regimes) that he formulated the "law" or observation, so as to call attention to the fact that frivolous use of such analogies tends to "rob the valid comparisons of their impact."

He is particularly critical of Holocaust comparisons: "*Although deliberately framed as if it were a law of nature or*

Godwin's Law

of mathematics, its purpose has always been rhetorical and pedagogical: I wanted folks who glibly compared someone else to Hitler or to Nazis to think a bit harder about The Holocaust." A perfect example of this is in the recent tendency of trafficking fanatics to brand those who question their wild exaggerations as the equivalent of Holocaust deniers: To compare the ancient evil of slavery with the modern one of genocide is merely asinine, but to compare those who demand basic proof for extraordinary claims with fanatics who deny overwhelming physical and documentary evidence and thousands of eyewitness accounts, is both highly hypocritical and astonishingly irrational.

But Godwin's clear statements about the intended application of his "law" don't prevent some people from attempting to censor others' arguments by invoking it even when the comparisons it is leveled against are in fact valid. What makes such misuse more worthy of note than other sleazy argumentation tactics is what it says about people's perception of the Nazi phenomenon: By pretending the Nazis were so evil that *no* comparison to them, however apt, is reasonable, we essentially say that Nazism was some sort of fluke that could never happen again...and that, sadly, is completely untrue. People tend to overlook the fact that the Nazis were a legitimate political party duly elected to leadership of an advanced, modern country by the exact same democratic process as leaders are elected in every Western nation today. Hitler was not a military dictator who seized power in some bloody *coup d'état* but a politician whose party came into power by popular vote, and all of his actions as chief executive were 100% legal under the laws enacted by the German legislature. The Nazis came to power by the same means as politicians always come to power everywhere (namely by telling the people what they wanted to hear), and the German people accepted the militaristic oppression of the Nazis for the exact reason that the British and American people have accepted the abridgement of their civil rights and ever-expanding police powers: they valued the illusion of "safety" over the reality of liberty.

What this means is that whatever we may think of the Nazis' *morality*, it's impossible to fault their *legality*. Morals are principles which transcend human behavior, while laws are merely arbitrary rules invented by eminently-fallible humans in order to control others and/or impose their own personal views of right action. Some laws are moral and many immoral, but the majority are simply amoral; however, even moral or amoral laws can be (and often are) used for the highly immoral purpose of exerting external control over inoffensive individuals who neither desire nor require that control. And because this is so, the act of agreeing to serve as a police operative in *any* regime is at best an amoral one, because in doing so the individual agrees to enforce (by violence or threat thereof) *all* of the laws passed by his government, whether he agrees with them or not; he abdicates his personal morality to those in authority and allows his actions to be dictated by others, even if he knows those actions to be wrong.

At Nuremberg, Western society established the legal precedent that "I was only following orders" is not a valid defense against wrongdoing even if the offender was only a low-level functionary in an authoritarian system. Yet how often do we hear police abuses (especially against whores) defended with phrases like "they're just doing their job" or "cops don't make the laws, they just enforce them"? If a cop is tasked with enforcing a law he knows to be immoral, it is his duty as a moral man to refuse that order even if it means his job. If he agrees with an immoral law then he is also immoral, and if he enforces a law he knows to be wrong even more so. The law of the land in Nazi-era Germany was for Jews and other "undesirables" to be sent to concentration camps, and the maltreatment of the prisoners was encouraged and even ordered by those in charge; any German soldier or policeman enforcing those laws was the exact moral equivalent of any soldier or policeman under any other democratically-elected government enforcing the laws enacted by that regime. Either "I was only following orders" is a valid defense, or it isn't; either we agree that hired enforcers are absolved from responsibility because "they're just doing their jobs", or we don't. You can't have it both ways, and sometimes Nazi analogies are entirely appropriate.

A Necessary Evil

Government is not reason. Government is not eloquence. It is force. And, like fire, it is a dangerous servant and a fearful master. – George Washington

If I told you that an evil action became less evil with increasing numbers of participants, you would think me either mad or morally deficient; after all, we tend to view the actions of criminal gangs with, if anything, even *more* horror than the crimes of individuals. But the truth is that most people subscribe to a repugnant form of moral relativism in which evil actions, no matter how reprehensible, magically

15

become "good" once those actions are agreed upon by "authorities" and sanctified by some ceremony involving sacred rituals, holy words, blessed costumes and (most importantly) baptism under euphemisms that cloak their true character.

Nearly everyone who isn't a sociopath would agree that an individual who harms another commits a wrong; most of us also accept the existence of certain mitigating circumstances which might *excuse* such a wrongful action, such as killing in self-defense. And most of us would probably also agree that the violence was still regrettable, and therefore a thing to be avoided without serious provocation; the wrongful action never becomes actually good, but it can become a defensible, acceptable or even necessary evil. In any case, the factor which moderates the act is the *motive*, not the number of people who commit it: a wrong committed by two people, ten people, forty thousand people or three hundred million people is still a wrong, even if a majority of them agree to commit it; only a vital need can ameliorate the evil. No motive, however pure, and no consensus, however large, can fully transform an evil act into a good one; the best we can hope for is that nobody involved could see a better alternative at the time.

Some people wish to deny that this is so; they claim that if a majority of the inhabitants of a place agree that an evil action isn't evil, then it isn't. The trouble with this argument is that those who make it never *really* believe it. They won't declare that slavery was right and good through most of human history, or that it's moral to slaughter those who won't agree to follow a conqueror's religion, or that heretics and homosexuals should be burned at the stake and deformed babies set out to die…even though all of those ideas (and many others equally abominable) were accepted by majorities, often overwhelming majorities, in the cultures which practiced them. If you're going to argue that confiscation of the property of unpopular citizens, or the abduction and enslavement of others, or the abrogation of some people's rights, or the overruling of some people's choices, are OK for the "greater good", you had better also be prepared to sign off on enslavement, torture, lynchings, purges, pogroms and genocide, all of which were sanitized by the same monstrous excuse in many times and places over at least the past six millennia.

It's fascinating in a train-wreck sort of way to watch the spastic mental dance people perform in order to get around this grim equation; they declare that "democracy" excuses collectively-committed crimes (except of course for those committed by other people's "democracies"), ignoring the fact that our ancestors assigned the same divine right to their kings that moderns assign to the majority. Or they make childish pronouncements about "The Law", as though it had been handed down by an omniscient sky-deity on stone tablets in full view of assembled Humanity and was renewed unchanged and inviolate in every generation since we climbed down from the trees. Some of them will even enthusiastically condemn any and every social grouping – families, gangs, fraternities, corporations, religions, political parties and even local governments – for their sins and abuses, yet declare their national government (or, even more bizarrely, the United Nations) a positive good.

A government is just a group of people, selected by some arbitrary means according to some arbitrary rules agreed upon by some group powerful enough to impose its own views on the rest of the population without instantly

17

triggering revolution. That's all it is, and it doesn't have any special Divine Right to make decisions for everybody else. As Washington pointed out, a government has no power to enforce its decrees except via threat of violence, and that automatically makes it an evil no matter what the motivations of those who control it. This does not mean Mankind can do wholly without government at this stage in our evolution; far from it. One would have to be a naive fool to believe that a *completely* anarchistic society could long survive without degenerating into chaos; however, it would be equally foolish to declare that dressing thugs in interesting costumes and giving them fancy titles makes them anything but thugs, and that calling "might makes right" by euphemisms such as "law enforcement" and "the justice system" somehow makes it moral.

My point is not that we should abolish government entirely; it is that our love affair with it, and our passive acceptance of the lie that it is good and holy, endanger every living thing on Earth and imperil the continued survival of Western culture. Oncologists and cancer patients are under no illusion about the destructiveness of chemotherapy; they recognize it as a poisonous, dangerous procedure only slightly better than the illness it treats. I daresay nearly everyone would be happy to abandon it as an obsolete barbarity were there a better and less destructive therapy available, and I cannot imagine any sane physician's enthusiastically supporting the use of it for other diseases, especially not non-terminal ones. But with government it's the exact opposite; many people seem to consider it the solution for every problem, and deny its danger despite ample evidence to the contrary. We would rightfully distrust a physician who lied about the danger of chemotherapy, who insisted on giving the patient as many sessions as possible whether necessary or not, and who prescribed it for every ailment from bullet wounds to insomnia; yet, we accept the word of career politicians who make the same sort of claims about government. Right now, government is the most widely-accepted way to secure individual rights and prevent oppression of the weak by the strong, just as chemotherapy is the most widely-accepted means of combating cancer. But neither of them is a *good* solution, and until we can find something better both must be used as warily and sparingly as possible lest they inflict more harm than the ailments they were intended to remedy.

The Daughters of Shamhat

She was not ashamed to take him, she made herself naked and welcomed his eagerness; as he lay on her murmuring love she taught him the woman's art. For six days and seven nights they lay together, for Enkidu had forgotten his home in the hills; but when he was satisfied he went back to the wild beasts. Then, when the gazelle saw him, they bolted away; when the wild creatures saw him they fled. Enkidu would have followed, but his body was bound as though with a cord, his knees gave way when he started to run, his swiftness was gone. And now the wild creatures had all fled away; Enkidu was grown weak, for wisdom was in him, and the thoughts of a man were in his heart. – *The Epic of Gilgamesh* (Tablet I)

The Essential Maggie McNeill

While I understand why many activists and allies argue decriminalization from human rights, libertarian or harm reduction viewpoints, and indeed use these arguments myself because they are all valid ones, it's sad that almost nobody wants to acknowledge another, equally important factor: human society needs whores every bit as much as it needs farmers, soldiers, physicians and builders, and far more than it needs preachers, academic feminists, politicians and 90% of the other control freaks who work so assiduously at rousing the rabble against us. Our ancient ancestors understood this; it's not accidental that in the *Epic of Gilgamesh*, the temple harlot Shamhat is the one who tames the wild man Enkidu, turning him from a beast to a man. But in the 5000 years since that powerful myth was first pressed into clay, Man's world has forgotten its debt to us and has generally succumbed to the hubris of believing it no longer needs us; even in areas where our trade is legalized or decriminalized there is the self-important pretense that we are merely being tolerated as a magnanimous landlord might allow stray cats to eke out a marginal living on his property. The change was very gradual; it wasn't until about half the time between the writing of *Gilgamesh* and that of this essay had elapsed that someone first conceived of the idea of bringing the civilizing power of whores under the control of the state. As discussed in one of my earliest essays, the Athenian politician Solon passed laws to reduce the relatively high status of Greek wives, and attempted to undermine the power of both independent prostitutes and the cult of Aphrodite by establishing cheap state-run brothels staffed by Asian slave girls; the failure of his attempt is a demonstration of the futility of proposals by certain historically-ignorant academics to establish a similar system with machines in place of slaves (*see page 102*). The Romans, Japanese,

20

The Daughters of Shamhat

Catholic Church and other powers of the next two millennia did not even attempt to replicate Solon's scheme, but rather contented themselves with taxing, regulating and socially isolating whores in order to establish patriarchal dominance while still allowing us to perform our vital social function: giving men, whose demand (as Camille Paglia put it) "always exceeds the female supply," an outlet for that surplus libido.

Wise whores all know what feminists, preachers, politicians and pundits vociferously deny: our trade saves far more marriages than it endangers, by allowing men the sexual variety they crave without endangering the social, emotional and economic arrangements of marriage. In fact, I would even say that it was the emergence of commercial prostitution in the first millennium BCE which made widespread monogamy feasible; I predict that an historical study would reveal that few if any cultures abandoned polygamy before hookers were widespread in that society. Nor are wives the only women whose safety and happiness are protected by harlots; prior to the late 19th century everyone from saints to kings understood that whores allow male passions which might lead to rape or other unsavory sexual behaviors to be siphoned off harmlessly in a manner which helps support some women while simultaneously preventing harm to others. A number of studies (several of them archived on my blog's Resources page) have shown that the rates of rape and other sex crimes decrease in societies where prostitution is decriminalized or otherwise tolerated, and Swedish statistics document a sharp rise in rape after the implementation of their much-vaunted client criminalization model.

In some parts of the world, prostitution is already widely viewed as a job like any other, and most non-totalitarian governments recognize the need for our trade despite a refusal to publicly acknowledge it; even the United States pointedly ignores the existence of most escort services (and prior to the rise of "sex trafficking" hysteria, massage parlors) except for periodic raids designed to "keep us in our place" and to please moralistic authoritarians. Some very limited groups (such as the more educated and/or wise among both sex workers and clients, the majority of sex therapists and some advocates for the disabled [*see page 9*]) already recognize the vital role whores play in human society, and I can envision a future (depicted in my story "Necessity", in *Ladies of the Night*) where even most governments understand it at least as well as they did for most of history. But for now, I'll have to content myself with urging activists and allies to stop ceding ground to prohibitionists by pretending that prostitution is an evil to be tolerated rather than a good to be celebrated.

The Birth of a Movement

NOS ENFANTS NE VEULENT PAS LEUR MERE EN PRISON. – Banner hung on the front of St. Nizier's, June 2nd, 1975

Contrary to the perceptions of Americans and others, the French have been unusually intolerant of working-class prostitution for centuries. About the middle of the 16th century a moral panic over the new venereal disease, syphilis, swept across Europe (*see page 71*); then, as now, prostitutes

The Birth of a Movement

were blamed for diseases spread mostly by promiscuous amateurs, and despite arguments from theologians and philosophers that prostitution was a necessary social safety valve, French moral crusaders demanded that it be "abolished" by closing brothels and arresting streetwalkers (*Plus ça change, plus c'est la même chose!*) Since they catered to the needs of the upper class, courtesans were naturally ignored; it was only the whores who were available to the middle and lower classes who were suppressed. Streetwalkers were periodically rounded up and thrown in jail or deported to the colonies (*see page 195*), while brothels owned by the wealthy and/or well-connected arranged private deals to be tolerated, becoming the *maisons closes* which characterized French prostitution up until the aftermath of World War II. Brothels owned by poorer madams managed to stay open by bribing the police with money and sex...and I need not tell you that venerable system is still alive in many countries to this day.

Things went on like this for over 200 years, until the Revolution and its consequent social upheavals drove huge numbers of women into prostitution for survival. The *bourgeois* had fits and demanded that "something be done", so under the *Code Napoleon* police were given the power to "control" the trade. In Paris, the world's first vice squad (the *police des moeurs*) was organized; its job was to register all whores and to require them to submit to monthly health inspections (at the women's cost, of course); if a woman was found to be infected, or failed to show up on time, or was unable to pay her fee, or had failed to pay whatever bribes or provide whatever sex was demanded by the cops, she was confined to a "prison hospital" until the "authorities" decided to let her go. Registered prostitutes were oppressed by an ever-increasing number of rules about where, when, how and with whom they could work; by 1830 these regulations had become so stringent there was literally no way to obey them and still make a living, nor was there any right of appeal for any cop's pronouncement because there were no actual laws on prostitution (just police rules made up by the police and enforced at their discretion). The only way to avoid all this was to work in one of the *maisons closes*, but they were just as bad because one of the conditions for a license was that any cop had unrestricted access to any occupant of such a house at all times. Furthermore, the police demanded such huge bribes and fees from the madams that they in turn had to extract more money from the girls.

Unsurprisingly, most women preferred to risk working illegally than to submit to this regime, so the police took it upon themselves to decide which women were prostitutes; any lower-class woman seen walking alone, or noticed in the company of different men at different times, or accused by an enemy, was arrested and forcibly registered as a "known prostitute" for the rest of her life. This was the soil from which the modern pimp first sprung; since men could move about freely, they could seek clients for women who wanted to steer clear of the police. A whore accompanied by a pimp in public could pass as a "respectable" woman, and male lookouts could warn groups of streetwalkers to hide when the police approached. Whores learned to move in and out of different brothels, to change residences, cities and even names, and to employ pimps to avoid detection; by the dawn of the Social Purity Era in the 1870s the French system was moribund, and panic over "clandestine prostitution" fed on the same white middle-class Christian women's frustration over their inability to control everyone else's sexuality that soon gave rise to an avalanche of anti-prostitution laws in the United States.

But while the moral crusaders of America and Britain imagined they could completely abolish prostitution, the French would not succumb to that delusion for several generations yet. Instead, they became obsessed with an "epidemic of lesbianism" in the *maisons closes* and blamed police regulation for the ills of prostitution, demanding that the system be dismantled. In 1907 that was indeed done, but the police maintained surveillance of whores under the pretext of "maintaining public order"; this was accomplished in part by using threats to secure the cooperation of cheap hotels (*maisons de rendezvous*) where streetwalkers took their clients. Thus the public believed that the regulation system had ended, when in fact it had merely become sneakier. This state of affairs continued until World War II, which resulted in a wave of anti-whore propaganda culminating in France's being declared officially "abolitionist" in 1960 (*see "Collaboration Horizontale" in Volume II*). The old registries were destroyed, but as always the police became even worse with increased criminalization. By 1974, the embattled French hookers had enough; the police had (as usual) done nothing about two mutilation murders of prostitutes in Lyon, so a group of whores and supporters (including lawyers and journalists) called a protest meeting to demand an end to the various anti-prostitute laws and police repression which was endangering their lives by forcing them to work in dark, sparsely-trafficked areas. The police responded by harassing the protesters with three or four fines per day each, and the French tax authorities made ridiculous estimates of the number of clients each protesting worker saw, then presented them with tax bills exceeding their entire incomes. When they appeared on television to tell the public what was happening, they were sentenced to prison *in absentia* for the unpaid fines and taxes. Seeing that dramatic action was called for, on Monday, June 2nd, 1975 a group of over 100 prostitutes occupied the Church of St. Nizier in Lyon with the cooperation of the priest; they hung a banner across the front of the building stating in French, "OUR CHILDREN DON'T WANT THEIR MOTHERS IN PRISON."

When the government responded by threatening to take their children away if they did not leave immediately, there was a public outcry; many women of Lyon joined them so the cops would be unable to tell which were prostitutes. Furthermore, the *demimonde* of Paris dispatched a delegation to assist them, groups in other parts of France also occupied churches, and a "prostitutes' strike" was organized in several provinces. The protest went on for a week, and ended predictably: at 5:30 AM on Tuesday, June 10th, cops tricked the priest into unlocking a door which they then forced open, allowing dozens of thugs in riot gear to invade the building. All of the occupying whores were beaten and arrested, and similar actions were carried out over the next few days at all the other protest sites; by Friday the 13th it was over.

But if the "authorities" imagined their brutal suppression of a peaceful protest would teach the lesson they had intended, they were sadly mistaken; the whores began holding regular meetings and soon formed the French Collective of Prostitutes, on which the English Collective of Prostitutes was later modeled. Women in a number of other countries were also inspired to form groups, and a number of these came together with Margo St. James' COYOTE to form the International Committee for Prostitutes' Rights

The Birth of a Movement

(ICPR), the organization whose work and example helped to win prostitution law reform in a number of European countries and provided an example which inspired similar campaigns in many other parts of the world. In a way, the modern sex worker rights movement was born on that June 2nd in Lyon, so we celebrate it now as International Whores' Day. Many victories have been won in the years since that first lost battle, but we still have a long way to go until our profession is recognized as legitimate and governments cease to treat us as cattle to be herded and milked as they please. In the past two decades the prohibitionists have succeeded in forcing us into a defensive posture via their "sex trafficking" mythology and tyranny wrapped up in "feminist" garb, but all moral panics inevitably end and most young women are not threatened by sex as the current feminist establishment is. The tide of history is toward greater individual rights, and those who would restrict others' sexuality, no matter what propaganda they employ, will eventually be swept away.

The Fourth of July

Ee'd plebnista norkohn forkohn perfectunun...
– Cloud William (Roy Jenson) in "The Omega Glory"

Even when *Star Trek* was bad, it could have moments that were memorable and said something important. In the deeply-flawed episode "The Omega Glory", descendants of early Earth colonists (or else the inhabitants of an impossibly parallel world) fought a bacteriological war between

27

Americans and Chinese which ended in both nations being hurled back into barbarism; the Yangs (Yankees) still have an American flag and a copy of the Constitution, but have forgotten the real meaning of the artifacts. They revere the flag as a totem and recite the "holy words" by rote; the epigram is the Yang leader's rendition of the beginning of the Preamble to the Constitution ("We the People, in order to form a more perfect union…") altered by centuries of repetition without meaning. They live in a tribal culture ruled by chiefs and elders, practice trial by combat, and adhere to a code of religious law completely at odds with the sacred documents they can no longer read. To them, "freedom" is nothing but a "worship word" forbidden to infidels, and the Constitution is taboo for the eyes of anyone but a chief.

The situation presents a useful (if exaggerated) metaphor of modern America; though we have not descended to the barbarism of the Yangs, our law and traditions have drifted ever further from their philosophical & constitutional moorings. The Founding Fathers would not recognize the current legal code of this country, grounded as it is in religion and other dangerous superstitions and "-isms" inimical to the Enlightenment philosophy and thousand-year-old English common law tradition in which it was originally based. Our chiefs and priests of the law claim to revere the Constitution yet violate it at every turn; their sycophantic followers proclaim that interpretation of the "holies" is only for the elite, and rabble like us need merely obey "just authority". And though "freedom" is still a "worship word" in this country, observing the ovine obsequiousness with which Americans submit to looting, sexual molestation, brutality and demands of literal obeisance to petty officials leads me to the unavoidable conclusion that they have as little

The Fourth of July

understanding of its meaning as the fictional Cloud William did. The title of this essay is the name by which most Americans refer to this day: not "Independence Day" to acknowledge the actual reason for the observance (a declaration by brave and principled men that they refused to submit to tyranny), but rather just a date on a calendar, an excuse to stay home from work and celebrate their dependence on the overlords who so graciously grant them the holiday.

The oath Cloud William called the *Ay Pledgli* ends with the words, "...with liberty and justice for all," and the pairing is not an arbitrary one: liberty and justice are inextricably bound together, and the only way to guarantee the one is to protect the other. When government actors are not only given greater rights and greater legal standing than other citizens, but are in fact insulated from the consequences of their own evil actions against others, the liberty of ordinary citizens becomes subject to the whims of those officials and justice dies. And when individuals, groups or institutions are allowed to commit injustices against others, how can the liberty of those so victimized survive? In trying to explain to the Yangs what their "holy words" really meant, Captain Kirk said, *"That which you call Ee'd Plebnista was not written for the chiefs or the kings or the warriors or the rich and powerful, but for all the people...not...only for the Yangs, but for the Kohms as well...they must apply to everyone or they mean nothing!"* Sometime in the past two centuries, Americans forgot that; individuals and groups used government as a means to deny liberty and justice to others, and thus created the machinery by which their own liberty was stolen. In the real world, there aren't any wise heroes

29

from outer space to come down and rescue us from our own decadence by explaining the meaning of our sacred truths; we're going to have to rediscover them for ourselves, without assistance from the stars. Liberty is both a blessing and a burden; justice is both a boon and a solemn duty. And if we continue to abdicate responsibility for both to the least evolved and most barbaric among us, we won't need a world war to destroy everything our ancestors built.

Advice for Clients

Treat a whore like a lady and a lady like a whore. – Wilson Mizner

This is not a list of my personal pet peeves, but rather commonsense advice and warnings against behaviors I know annoy most whores rather than those which just annoy me in particular.

Don't ask rude, stupid, pointless or prying questions, or those to which you don't really want to know the answer.

This could almost be an essay by itself; day after day we're asked the same questions which one would think men would have better sense than to ask, but obviously don't. My own pet peeve is, "Are you clean?" There's a persistent myth that sex workers are vectors of disease (*see page 71*), but that's completely untrue; the sex worker groups with the highest disease rates still have *half* the rate of promiscuous amateurs, and the more scrupulous pros enjoy an infection rate that's a miniscule fraction of that in the sexually-active segment of the general population. Just keep your eyes open and be as scrupulous as we are with condoms and you won't have to waste your time with this rude and pointless query. Then there's, "What's your real name?" If *she* wanted you to have it, don't you think she would've given it to you? Again, both rude and pointless.

If you live in a police state where our trade is suppressed (such as the US), a number of questions fall into this category, such as the amazingly stupid, "Are you a cop?" This derives from the myths about undercover cops (largely spread by drug users) which claim that there is some magic formula (*see page 166*) for detecting them. Nothing could be farther from the truth; a cop can lie, misrepresent himself, bring up the subject of sex first, take his socks off, or even shag a girl to completion and still bust her, and it won't ruin his case one atom because even if there *were* rules of this sort (which there usually aren't), he would just perjure himself and claim he didn't do whatever it was he wasn't supposed to do. If the supposed whore you're trying to pick up claims she isn't a cop, the statement is worth exactly what it cost her to make it: Zero. A similar question is, "Is this legal?" *How the hell is the girl supposed to answer that?* I mean really! "No, I'm a criminal?" All this question does is to make her uncomfortable and to cause her to wonder if she's being taped. An even worse (and unfortunately far more common) one is, "What do I get for my money?" If a girl ever answers this question with anything more specific than, "You get an hour of my time," you should suspect that *you're* being taped because no experienced girl worth the money would ever say anything else.

The last category includes such questions as, "How many men have you seen today?" or "Are you married?" or "Has anyone ever hurt you?" Maybe the real answers would turn you on, but they might turn you off, and your escort has no way of knowing which. You might very well *think* you want to know the answer, and then change your mind when you hear it. So it's best to avoid these kinds of questions in the first place, and if you ask something which the girl seems not to want to answer, don't press the issue.

Be clean.

Just that simple; give a professional the same respect you would give an amateur. Take a shower, shave, brush your teeth, cut your fingernails, and *please* for Aphrodite's sake wash your butt, including your anus, with soap. Change into clean clothes and refrain from smoking in her presence unless she is also a smoker or has ashtrays available to signify it's OK. If you're uncircumcised, clean the area under your foreskin thoroughly, and if you have any sort of skin condition please clean it properly and let her know what it is as soon as you disrobe. And if you see even the slightest sign of any kind of sexually transmitted disease, please seek medical attention immediately and do not even *attempt* to hire a girl until your doctor pronounces you clear!

Employ normal good manners.

I know proper etiquette is less common than it used to be, but c'mon guys, this isn't rocket science. Just try to remember all the things Mommy taught you; ask rather than demanding, say "thank you" at the end, answer the door in at *least* a bathrobe, take off your hat when a woman is in the

32

room, etc. You'll be surprised how much of a difference it makes in your experience.

Remember that we are businesswomen and that this is our business.

You wouldn't make a cashier have to ask for her money, and you shouldn't make us ask either; different girls want the money handed over in different ways, but most of us want it up front. Also, you wouldn't expect a plumber, exterminator or other professional to "hang out" with you off the clock after the job for which he was contracted was done. Good professionals try to create an exciting illusion for you; don't destroy it by forcing us to remind you that we're there for the money.

Be where you say you're going to be when you say you're going to be there.

If you're going to an incall, try to be on time (which does *not* mean early) and call if you'll be more than five minutes late; if the girl is coming to you, don't leave to go to the store, the ice machine, the front desk or the ATM when you expect her any minute. You should have done those things long before; if there is a real emergency, just call to tell her so she can delay arriving for the time it will take you to get back. And if there's a substantial delay which is your fault rather than hers, please don't be an ass if she cuts the session a bit short; she may have other appointments and she didn't force you to arrive half an hour later than expected. Finally, if you get cold feet please call to cancel, and if she's already on the way just face her like a man and pay her cancellation fee; she may have turned down other appointments to keep yours, and it isn't her fault you misplaced your balls at the last minute.

If receiving a date at your home or office, provide basic necessities.

One would think this would be obvious, but one would be wrong. A man who would never invite a social date or a business contact to a place without furniture, running water, air conditioning or heat may think nothing of inviting a business date to such a place. Here's a word of advice, guys: Next time, use the money to buy a bed or air conditioner or have water installed, or else find a place which already has those things.

Don't have anyone there who isn't participating.

You may simply want to show your friends the choice bit of tail you're about to enjoy, but she may find it very threatening to have a door opened to a room full of guys, even if they immediately file out as soon as she arrives. I've left calls (with the money) because drunk and/or obnoxious frat boys or convention attendees keep banging on the door, ringing the phone or trying to take my picture through the crack allowed before the chain stops the door, and so would any other girl with a particle of common sense or an iota of self-esteem. Arrange your liaisons when your friends won't be around, or if others will be there ask if it's OK up front (as in the case of a bachelor party). Also, I really don't care if your son or daughter is "too young to understand"; hire your whores on weekends when you *don't* have visitation, or at least find a babysitter for the time you need. We're not monsters out of Victorian propaganda, so having a child in the next room is very uncomfortable for many of us.

Don't try to turn her into a criminal.

If you ask her to bring drugs, she'll probably just hang up on you because cops love to get two busts for the price of one. And don't ask an agency girl to tell the agency you cancelled, then come to see you anyhow; not only is this dangerous for her since nobody will know where she is, but also puts her job at risk because the agency will fire her the second they find out she's stealing calls.

Keep your fingers outside of her body.

The average professional strongly dislikes having dirty, rough, bumpy fingers forcibly inserted (often without warning or lubrication) into her vagina, anus or even mouth. Even surgically clean fingers with nails trimmed down to the quick can be terribly uncomfortable, and once the man starts to wriggle them around violently it can become acutely painful. If you have a fetish for this please ask if it's OK before doing it, and abide by whatever answer you get.

Don't even *ask* to go without a condom.

Even though we hear it all the time, it doesn't mean it isn't annoying or even infuriating. If you want a whore to think of you as an imbecile or a fool, "Do I have to use a condom?" is the most effective way. If you want to insult her

35

at the same time, opt for "How much to do it without a condom?" instead.

Respect her limits.

Just because you've hired a girl to do a job does *not* make her your slave. If she tells you she doesn't "speak Greek", don't try to penetrate her anally. If she is uncomfortable with some fetish you didn't bother to warn her about, leave it alone. If she doesn't want to give you her phone number or let you take her picture, drop the subject. A professional is not some naive schoolgirl you can seduce into doing something against her will; all you're going to accomplish is annoying her and wasting the time you paid for, and if she feels threatened enough she will leave and you will be out your money with nothing to show for it.

Above all else, just apply common sense and common courtesy; scour every trace of the Madonna/whore duality and the myth of the wanton out of your mind and treat a sex worker as you would treat any other businesswoman and you can't go very wrong. You'll be the kind of client professionals like to see rather than the kind we dread, and you'll find your experience is much more rewarding and fulfilling because of it.

Enough is Enough

Going too far is as bad as not going far enough. –
Chinese proverb

Most people will probably agree that quality is more important than quantity, and most *reasonable* people recognize that it's possible to have too much of a good thing. But it seems very few people, especially in America, can resist the temptation to want more of something that was fine as it was. This isn't about portion size, though I suppose one could stretch the point to include that; what I'm really talking about is portion number.

The hero of C.S. Lewis' fantasy novel *Out of the Silent Planet*, Dr. Ransom, arrives via a series of adventures on Mars, whose inhabitants never "fell" and therefore still live in a state of grace. One of the Martians tells Ransom that his people cannot understand the human drive to keep repeating things; if a Martian has a pleasant experience, he appreciates it for what it was and feels no compelling need to do it over again. In fact, they feel that to repeat it too soon would actually cheapen the initial experience. Reading that was one of those moments in which a book has a profound effect on one's life; I had always felt exactly like Lewis' Martians, and had never understood why other people didn't. That passage gave me the words to describe how I felt, and let me know that I wasn't the only person on Earth who saw it that way.

Let me give you a few examples. Once Olivia told me that she liked a new album so much she had "put it on repeat all afternoon". I told her that I didn't think my CD player had such a function, and she replied that she suspected

37

it did but I just hadn't ever looked for it. As it turned out she
was exactly right; it had simply never occurred to me.
Though I do play favorite albums more often than others, I
literally could not comprehend why anyone would want to
play the same album over again immediately after listening to
it once. I was similarly flabbergasted by the kids who had
seen *Star Wars* dozens of times; though I like the movie, I've
probably seen it fewer times in my life than some of those
kids watched it in a month. It's the same thing with food
flavors: every time we went to my favorite Sno-Ball stand I
got a different flavor, and would never return to the same one
twice in a summer no matter how much I liked it; Jack, on
the other hand, got the same flavor (pralines and cream)
every single time we went there, without fail. The query,
"Don't you even want to *try* another flavor?" was invariably
answered with, "I like this one." I reckon that's why I
sympathize with the male need for sexual variety, even
though I don't feel it myself; on the other hand, I don't "get"
why anyone would want to have sex twice in a single hour.

As you can probably guess, I find Hollywood's
addiction to unnecessary sequels, remakes and "reboots"
incomprehensible. There are some movies which either need
or can smoothly accommodate sequels, and others which
can't; there are even some which practically scream, "Do not
cheapen me with a sequel!" (Rule of thumb: if the writers
can't think of an actual name and instead just call it "Such-
and-such II" it probably didn't need one). Sometimes it's
easy to tell; nothing short of physical force or a very large
sum of money could have compelled me to see *Highlander
II,* because though I loved *Highlander* I could clearly see
that the only way to make a sequel was to pervert the story.
Alas, I wasn't so perceptive when it came to *Ghostbusters II.*
The same thing goes for television shows; I truly respect

producers who end a show while it's still strong, rather than allowing it to "jump the shark" and degenerate into self-parody before finally limping to its grave. And I promise that if I ever feel my creative juices ebbing and recognize that the quality of my blog is starting to slip, I'll have the wisdom to say "OK, that's enough," and go out on a high note.

And that brings me to my main point (yes, there is one): I feel the same way about lives as I do about shows. Even if a person has a happy life, even a *spectacular* life, everything has a point at which it's best for it to end. Change is natural; just because a person is aging or disabled due to disease or injury does not mean his life is necessarily worse than it was when he was young and hale. In fact, some people are actually *happier* after such a change of life, just as some sequels surpass the original. So I'm not saying there should be some specific point at which everyone hangs it up; some TV series are spent after three seasons, while others can carry on for seven or more. What I *am* saying is that I respect the wisdom of those who can see when it's time to go, and choose to leave this plane in a dignified manner of their own choosing rather than being dragged kicking and screaming across the threshold, pathetically clinging to life like the cast of *After MASH*. Furthermore, I think it's an abomination for tyrants to prevent people from doing so, even when their lives have degenerated into inescapable nightmares; an individual who does not own and control his own body is a slave, and self-determination includes the right to self-termination. Quality, as I said at the beginning, is far more important than quantity, and a successful life is judged by its character rather than by the number of years it endures.

Heart of Gold

It is possible that the percentage of honest and competent whores is higher than that of plumbers and much higher than that of lawyers. And enormously higher than that of professors. – Robert A. Heinlein

Have you ever played that parlor game where someone names a category (like "animals" or "cheeses") and everyone tries to figure out which one you are? Like, "if you were a tree, which kind of tree would you be?" Well, we were playing this one night at UNO and someone chose the category "archetypal characters"; it took all of thirty seconds for everyone to agree that I was "the hooker with a heart of gold". For those unfamiliar with this archetype, she is a woman (sometimes an actual prostitute but not always) who by the sexual conventions of her society is "bad" or "immoral" or "sinful", but is actually a kind and virtuous person. The fact that this character has appeared in literature since at least Roman times shows that at least on some level many humans recognize that a woman's willingness to comply with her society's sexual mores has little to do with her actual morality. One can always tell how well a writer comprehends this truth by the way in which he uses such a character; if he depicts her as miserable and fallen and forced into prostitution by circumstances or poverty or a pimp, he obviously does believe that sex truly is bad and dirty and therefore his heroine cannot have willingly entered harlotry. But if he depicts her as an unrepentant whore who makes no excuses for her profession and yet still is good and noble, it is because he recognizes the arbitrary nature of any given society's sexual rules and therefore understands that virtuous

40

whores, as Heinlein points out, are far more common than virtuous individuals in many "respectable" professions.

Most reading this probably recognize that the latter depiction of the "tart with a heart" is the truer one; I can honestly say that the moral composition of the population of sex workers in any given area basically resembles the moral composition of the population in general. There are honest whores and dishonest whores, moral and immoral ones, generous ones and greedy ones, ones who help their sisters and ones who will stab them in the back to make an extra fifty bucks…just like any other people. Despite what cops and bluenoses like to claim, hookers are no more inclined to criminality than anyone else; the way some of these ignorant jackasses talk, they make it sound as though if our trade were decriminalized most would leave it in droves to find some illegal way to make a living! While it's true that some marginalized sex workers will steal from customers, it's because they're poor and desperate; some hotel maids and minimum-wage retail employees do the same thing for the same reason, but I don't see anyone calling for those professions to be prohibited. And yes, even some not-so-marginalized escorts try to scam their customers for more money; do you honestly believe some mechanics, doctors and lawyers don't do the same thing? Refusing to obey the arbitrary sexual rules of society does not make whores any more "corrupt" or "evil" than it does queers or kinksters for the same reason, and though many promiscuous amateurs are far more unscrupulous than pros (because they lack our professional ethics), I'll bet the average moral imbecile would consider it the other way around!

The Essential Maggie McNeill

Once Linda said to me, "Maggie, you're so beautiful and so smart, you could easily take these men for a lot more than you do."

I replied, "That's as may be, but I can sleep at night." Yes, as whores go I was unusually honest, but then I'm unusually honest for a woman, a person, an American, a writer or any other group I happen to be a member of. My innate honesty has nothing to do with my profession; it existed long before I ever accepted money for sex, and did not lessen merely because I gave up one profession for another. My girls all knew that I frowned on dishonesty, so dishonest girls never lasted long at my agency and those who (like most people) might be tempted to occasional "fudging" were discouraged from doing so by my attitude. Yet, I never had any trouble finding girls to work for me, which tells me that escorts are no more or less honest than anyone else.

I think my readers can probably tell that besides being honest, I also have a generous nature; as one of my friends once put it, "When Maggie does well everybody does well." She meant that when I can afford it I am never stingy with gifts, loans, picking up tabs, tipping, or anything else. As with honesty I'm not alone among whores in that respect; I've known a number of sex workers to go broke helping out their families and friends, and both my own experience and that of waitresses I've known informs me that most higher-income sex workers are usually big tippers. I think part of that is due to our knowing what it's like to be dependent on the generosity of patrons, but part of it has to be personality-driven because I've known some very wealthy people who were terrible tippers, and though generous with money they already have, few strippers have any scruples about hustling their customers for more to replace it.

42

Heart of Gold

Now, I'm not going to go into detail about the "hooker with a heart of gold" archetype; if you're interested in reading more about it I suggest you look up the Wikipedia article or the one at *TV Tropes and Idioms*, both of which feature numerous examples. I feel it only fair to warn you, however, that the latter site can be extremely addictive, and since both sites feature user-generated content the quality of the examples can vary widely; the *TV Tropes* article in particular has some commentary which demonstrates bias, acceptance of stereotypes and subscription to "pimps and traffickers" hysteria on the part of the writers. For the purposes of this article, all I need point out is that whether the character is major or minor and whether the writer allows her to live "happily ever after" (as in *Pretty Woman*) or feels compelled to redeem her by killing her off (as in *Camille*) says more about the writer and his intended audience than it does about actual hookers, golden-hearted or otherwise.

Because the very fact that a writer uses such a character in the first place shows that he (at least on some level) recognizes his society's sexual rules as arbitrary, the most important factor in determining how she will end up is not how he feels about those rules, but rather how he feels about women breaking them. Even in places and times when our trade is not sub-legal, whores are by our very nature nonconformists: by refusing to meekly submit to one man, by refusing to toil and spin, by refusing to be ashamed of our sexuality, by demanding cash for our favors rather than allowing men to sweet-talk us into giving them up, and by profiting from the male tendency toward promiscuity rather than whining or throwing tantrums over it, we violate every expectation of patriarchal society. Men are either fascinated by our charms or hate us for our power over them (or both); women are either jealous of our freedom or horrified by our courage (or both), and society as a whole refuses to openly accept us, yet would collapse into chaos without us.

By giving his character a "heart of gold" the writer represents her as a good person whose only fault is her refusal to accept the yoke expected of women, therefore her eventual fate demonstrates his belief about what will or should happen to people (especially women) who violate arbitrary standards. If she dies, we can be sure that the writer either believes that "you can't fight the system" (even if that system is unjust and wrong), or else that female willfulness is a tragic flaw which will destroy even an otherwise-virtuous woman. If she is "redeemed" through the actions of the hero, it's clear the writer feels that though unconventionality in women is a sin, it is not a mortal one and therefore can be forgiven if the poor deluded wretch sees the error of her ways and happily becomes the property of some man. But the rare example in which the virtuous whore both survives and yet remains unrepentant is indicative of a truly liberal attitude on the part of the writer: by allowing his symbol of noble nonconformity to triumph without recantation, he tells us not only that he believes in a woman's right to self-ownership, but also that he recognizes that arbitrary social conventions have no more resemblance to real morality than pantomime horses have to thoroughbreds.

The Source

When drinking water, think of its source.
– Chinese proverb

Of all the myths spread by prohibitionists about sex work, the most absurd and damaging is probably the claim that the average age of debut in sex work is about 13. The idea is farcical on its face; if the "average age" of a given group of people is 13, that means that (roughly speaking) for every 14-year-old in the group there is a 12-year-old, for every 17-year-old a 9-year-old, etc. In other words, if the "average age at which a girl enters prostitution" were really 13, for every woman who started at 25 there would be someone who started at 1. Obviously, this isn't exact; one 40-year-old could also be balanced by nine 10-year-olds, but I honestly don't think even the trafficking fanatics believe that kind of age imbalance could possibly exist.

A number of actual studies, including an informal survey I conducted of hundreds of sex workers, put the average age of entry as actually about 25. Even among underage prostitutes, the average age of entry is really about 16, so how in the world did anyone arrive at the ludicrous figure of 13 (which is sometimes even more idiotically claimed as the average age of prostitutes rather than the age at which we start)? For a time I thought the Estes & Weiner study, the origin of the "300,000 trafficked children" myth, was the original source, but as it turns out that is not the case; several readers told me it is attributed by Melissa Farley to three sources: a 1982 study of 200 San Francisco street workers, "Victimization of Street Prostitutes" by M.H.

The Essential Maggie McNeill

Silbert and A.M. Pines; a 1985 study with an even more melodramatic name, "Children of the Night" by D. Kelly Weisberg; and "Oppression Disguised as Liberation" by Denise Gamache and Evelina Giobbe. The last was not a research paper but rather an obscure, unpublished "discussion paper" for a domestic violence conference in 1990 (which specifically attributes the figure to "Children of the Night"). Furthermore, all of Weisberg's data (such as it is) was obtained by averaging figures from two studies with different methodologies and methods of calculation (in other words, she compares apples to oranges); one of them is Silbert and Pines. This means Farley has engaged in duplicity right from the start by pretending her figures derive from three sources, when in fact there is only one. Some prohibitionists do appear to recognize this, because Silbert & Pines is the paper most often cited as the source of the "average age is 13" figure; interestingly, it also produced another popular bit of misinformation, the myth that 80% of prostitutes are coerced.

Since the article wasn't readily available online I asked my correspondent Mary Setterholm (one of those who pointed out the Farley attributions) if she could locate it for me. At the time, she was a Divinity student at Harvard who had done considerable research for anti-trafficking groups (including Swanee Hunt's "Demand Abolition") and had consistently worked to convince them of the necessity for eschewing sensationalized figures, agency denial, anti-sex worker rhetoric and "end demand" nonsense; she is one of the most thorough, honest and tireless researchers I know. After Herculean effort she was able to track down the Gamache/Giobbe paper, but what she found in investigating Silbert & Pines was even more interesting: it contained no statement *at all* of a particular starting age! The closest was the phrase, "*Almost all the juvenile prostitutes in the study*

The Source

(96%) were runaways before they began prostitution," which says nothing about an "average age". Mary was intrigued, so she kept digging; in the backend data she found several quotes from another Silbert & Pines article (published the same year) named "Entrance into Prostitution":

> ...Average age at which subjects had (first) sexual intercourse with a boyfriend was a mean x = 13.5. Of these 34% felt coerced or forced, either emotionally (29%) or else physically (5%). Although 66% reported no coercion involved, many of their open-ended comments suggested pressure...The average age of starting prostitution was 16.1...On the average, subjects were working regularly as prostitutes when they were 16.9...The eight months difference between the average age of starting prostitution (16.1) and the average age of working regularly (16.9) indicates a somewhat reluctant entrance into street life...

What this means is that the ultimate source of the "13" myth actually lists the same average age at entry as most other studies of underage streetwalkers, about 16; the only mention of the number 13 was the figure for first intercourse with a boyfriend. Now, it's possible that in their haste to find damning "evidence" some prohibitionists blurred the numbers together in their minds, but given Melissa Farley's skill at massaging figures to suit her purposes that did not ring true to me. I also remembered this passage from Dr. Calum Bennachie's complaint to the APA about Farley (available on my Resource page):

> ...Colleen Winn, who was briefly employed by Dr Melissa Farley while she was in New Zealand [wrote]..."I believe Melissa did state that Māori women were entering

prostitution as young as 9 years old. Part of my position as researcher on this study was to help to collate data as I viewed all the questionnaires. I did not see these figures in the study at all. However, there were two women who stated that their first sexual experience was at age 9."
Question 13 of the questionnaire reads: "How old were you when you had your first sexual experience of any kind?"... page 3 of [Farley's] research...states: "An adolescent...had been in prostitution since age of 9..." Clearly, the answer to question 13 was put across as though it were the answer to question 1...[which asked] "What age were you when you first started prostitution?"

In other words, Melissa Farley has been known to intentionally conflate first age of intercourse with age of entry into prostitution in other cases, so it is very likely she did exactly that when quoting from Silbert & Pines' data. The "average age of 13" myth, repeated nigh-constantly by prohibitionists, "sex trafficking" fetishists and yellow journalists alike, is thus revealed as nothing more than a lie created through intentional (and tripled) misquotation of a methodologically-unsound more-than-30-year-old study, perpetrated by a charlatan working to advance her anti-sex agenda by any means necessary.

Ignoble Experiment

Beware of purity workers...ready to accept and endorse any amount of coercive and degrading treatment of their fellow creatures in the fatuous belief that you can oblige human beings to be moral by force. – Josephine Butler

At exactly 4:31 PM Eastern Time on December 5th, 1933, the 21st Amendment to the US Constitution was ratified, repealing the 18th Amendment and thus putting an end to the horribly-misnamed "Noble Experiment", a massive social engineering effort which cost the United States over $1 billion (over $13 billion in today's money) and resulted in the imprisonment, impoverishment and death of over 100,000 Americans. But despite the enormous economic and social costs (clogged courts, the rise of large-scale organized crime, widespread disrespect for all law, warfare in the streets and the birth of the modern police state, to name but a few), prohibitionists fought tooth and nail to prevent the dismantling of their mad scheme. Furthermore, politicians learned the wrong lesson from the experience: not "prohibition doesn't work and has catastrophic effects on society," but rather "start small and then slowly ratchet up the number and popularity of banned substances and behaviors, and spread prohibition across many bureaucratic regulations instead of investing it in one easily-targeted law."

I've often discussed the nearly-exact resemblance between "sex trafficking" hysteria and "white slavery" hysteria; I've also compared the rhetoric of sex work prohibitionists to that of drug prohibitionists, and I won't insult your intelligence by presuming any of y'all haven't recognized the resemblance between alcohol prohibition and

49

drug prohibition. But even though I've often said "All prohibitionism is the same," I wonder if y'all have ever given any thought to how *much* the same the various colors of prohibition are. Here are a few facts about the capital-P Prohibition whose end we rightfully celebrated; I won't waste my time and yours in pointing out the modern parallels, because they really are that obvious an exercise in *plus ça change.*

To prohibitionists, human rights, happiness and even life are subsidiary to "sending a message", and the cost of that message can never be too great. Various penalties proposed for the "crime" of drinking included torture, whipping, branding, imprisonment in Alaskan concentration camps, sterilization, enforced celibacy and even execution; some wanted the punishments applied to drinkers' children, grandchildren and even great-grandchildren. Others plotted to execute drinkers stealthily by releasing poisoned alcohol through undercover agents posing as bootleggers; they understood that the death toll could be in the hundreds of thousands, but declared that a "price worth paying" for an alcohol-free society. And though that plan was not carried out, the government *did* intentionally poison industrial alcohol in a failed attempt to keep people from drinking it; over 10,000 people died as a result. Police and G-men raided homes and businesses (often without warrant), seized or destroyed property (including cash, vehicles and buildings), murdered citizens and even crossed into Canada for their "operations". Nor were these depredations limited to government actors; prohibitionists formed groups to "assist" enforcement by spying on others, ratting them out to the police and even conducting raids on their own (*see page 59*).

Since the very real threat of official violence was still not enough to stop Americans from imbibing, prohibitionists

50

mounted a campaign of disinformation, sometimes producing bogus studies to "prove" their dogma. They claimed that any amount of drinking dramatically increased the chance of dying from edema, and that habitual drunks often died of spontaneous combustion. Drinking mothers (or even fathers) supposedly produced babies who were born addicted, and even the smell of alcohol was said to cause birth defects; some claimed these birth defects were inheritable, thus affecting multiple generations. Children were subjected to presentations "proving" that alcohol caused severe brain damage. The "anti-saloon" crowd also indulged in historical revisionism, censoring, reinterpreting or even retranslating documents (especially the Bible) to remove references to wine or other forms of alcohol, and altering pictures to retroactively turn historical figures into teetotalers.

The *soi-disant* Progressives wanted to remake society along "scientific" lines, to impose their idea of clockwork "perfection" on the human race; eugenics was a large part of this, as should be evident in the suggestion that "undesirables" be sterilized or their children executed with them. But though the Nazis gave eugenics such a bad name it was eliminated from "progressive" philosophy, the rest of its catechism is virtually untouched; neither Prohibition nor the decades-long "War on Drugs" has cured the adherents of that revolting 19th-century cult of their dedication to the idea that, as Butler put it, "any amount of coercive and degrading treatment" of peaceful citizens is acceptable in order to force them to obey the cultists' perverse notions of morality.

Not for Everybody

A dream to some; a nightmare to others.
– Merlin (Nicol Williamson) in *Excalibur*

Prostitution is completely natural female behavior; it actually predates marriage in human development (*see page 169*) and similar behaviors appear even in non-primate species. Most women will not hesitate to use their "erotic capital" (as Catherine Hakim calls it) to get ahead, and many have no qualms about openly using sex for material gain. Roughly 10% of all women have directly taken money for sex at least once, and about 1% have actually worked as prostitutes at some time in their lives. As George Bataille put it, "Not every woman is a prostitute, but prostitution is the natural apotheosis of the feminine attitude"; in other words, full-time professional prostitution occupies one end of a whole spectrum of behaviors on which it is impossible to draw a line separating the whore from the non-whore.

Obviously, less than 5% of all women (the historical percentage of the female population involved in the trade at any given time) feel comfortable enough with formal, professional prostitution to be able to actually make a living at it; it's even possible that some women, who feel drawn to the profession from an early age as I did, might actually be genetically predisposed to it. In other words, there might be a "hooker gene", and harlotry might be a sexual orientation no less than queerness or kink. The comparison is an apt one: just as some men find ecstasy in homosexual activity while others are utterly repulsed by it, so for some women whoring is a dream job while others find it a total nightmare.

52

Not for Everybody

Those who claim that homosexuality is "unnatural" might be inclined to use the comparison to argue that prostitution is equally unnatural (despite this view flying in the face of facts); for those who are so tempted, let me point out that motherhood is as natural a role for women as one could ever imagine, yet I doubt any sane person would disagree that there are some women who are totally unfit for it. No life-path or career is suitable for everyone, and as long as those who are unsuited to a given role avoid it there is no issue. But when a woman who is repulsed by motherhood becomes pregnant, or one who has difficulties dealing with people is forced into a job in which public contact is unavoidable, nobody should be surprised when serious problems ensue. And if a woman who dislikes men or has sexual hang-ups (or both) is forced by circumstance into prostitution, the result can be an unmitigated disaster.

I'm not talking about women who simply aren't cut out for whoredom; there are lots of those, which is why 10x as many women have tried hooking as have actually stuck with it for a time. The majority of women who directly take money for sex once or a few times simply decide it's not for them (for whatever reason) and find some other way to make a living. But there are a small number who should never have even tried it in the first place, yet are driven by necessity, desperation or actual coercion to practice it for weeks, months or even years; such women are among the worst enemies our profession ever had. Because they hate the work, they tend to see and remember only the negative aspects. And because many of them are emotionally damaged even before entering prostitution (due to whatever trauma caused them to hate men and/or sex), and virtually all of them became even more damaged by having to endure what for them was a loathsome existence, they either become fanatics on their own or are easily driven to fanaticism by the prohibitionists. These are the women who learn to "reframe their experiences" (i.e. lie to make their stories more lurid and to more closely conform to anti-whore rhetoric) and become what I call "professional survivors" ("survivor of prostitution" being the melodramatic prohibitionist term for an ex-whore). They are the mainstays of "john schools" and provide ammunition to prohibitionists, who represent their highly-embroidered claims as typical of sex work and even multiply the accounts by changing small details so as to make them sound like different-but-similar tales rather than one repeated *ad nauseum*. The very worst of them (as typified by disgraced "sex trafficking" icon Somaly Mam) are so obsessed with their own darkness that they are willing to utterly destroy the lives of any real human beings who get in the way of their quixotic crusades against private behavior that is literally impossible to eradicate as long as humans remain human.

In a world where individuals were allowed control over their own bodies and the decisions of adults (however strange those choices might seem to others) were always respected by the "authorities", fanatics who were harmed through ill-fortune or harmed themselves through their own poor choices would have no power over other, less damaged individuals. But unfortunately we do not yet live in such a world; even in jurisdictions where sex work is legal to one degree or another, governments believe they have the authority to abrogate the rights of individuals for whatever excuse strikes their collective fancy (provided they can convince the masses to lie still for it). As we saw in Rhode Island in 2009, a small group of vocal fanatics can easily convince the "authorities" to strip away rights held without challenge for decades, and one of the chief weapons of such fanatics is the emotionally-damaged "reluctant whore" who refuses to accept that her feelings or experiences are anything other than typical.

Straining at Gnats

Ye blind guides, which strain at a gnat, and swallow a camel. - Matthew 23:24

Sex worker rights activists hear a lot of arguments against decriminalizing our profession, absolutely none of them sound or reasonable (no matter what those who use them may believe). Most of them are based in one religion or another, and by religion I mean any belief system which is unsupported by (and may even fly in the face of) verifiable facts; others are rooted in the ever-popular desire to control women's sexuality, arguments that prostitution somehow causes harm to a nebulosity like "public decency", or the indefensible belief that personal aversions should be forced upon others at gunpoint. Some of these arguments are wholly ridiculous (*see page 130*), while others have the appearance of sensibility to those who are ignorant of either the realities of sex work or the inevitable and unintended consequences of any attempt to proscribe certain behaviors by the use of brute force; one of the most popular prohibitionist strategies of the past few decades falls into the latter category. Any advocate who presents a compelling moral, legal and practical case demonstrating categorically that decriminalization is better for everyone – sex workers, clients, families of both, health officials, society at large and even government treasuries – can be sure that once every other argument is defeated someone will intone sonorously, as though it were an unanswerable question, "But what about the trafficked children?" And though this one is no more valid than the others, its emotional impact often flusters even experienced advocates and triggers a reflexively apologetic stance which may well undermine everything she has previously said.

The most serious flaw in this line of attack (it cannot legitimately be called an argument) is the implication that decriminalization somehow harms coerced prostitutes, especially underage ones; in reality, nothing could be farther from the truth. When any business or consensual behavior is criminalized, the law lumps good people together with bad; a client who is kind and generous is equated with brutal or dishonest ones, an ethical escort service owner who treats her employees fairly is just as "criminal" as one who coerces workers and cheats clients, and so on. The primary tool of control for those who exploit women is not physical abuse, rape, drugs, or black magic as the various narratives pretend; it is threat of exposure to the "lawful authorities". Those present in a country without the requisite papers are subject to arrest, confinement and deportation, and in criminalization regimes like that of the United States just *being* a sex worker is illegal, so police are just as likely to arrest a coerced woman as one who adores her job. Clients or workers under decriminalization are free to report violence or suspected coercion to the police, while those under even partial criminalization are not due to fear of arrest. Furthermore, criminals are often attracted to criminality; in other words, those who are comfortable making a living outside the law are more likely to take advantage of the higher profits inherent in a black market, so that criminalizing any business actually attracts shady characters who might not otherwise be interested in it. Simply put, making sex work wholly or partially illegal tends to attract the sort of person who doesn't mind coercing others; make maid service illegal and there will almost certainly be a rise in the number of coerced, underage domestics.

Another thing that needs to be pointed out is that despite the claims of prohibitionists, the vast majority of sex workers are no more coerced than anyone else without a well-padded trust fund (*see page 145*); we all need to work, and we choose the work that suits us best (even if that work is highly unappealing to others). Less than 2% of all prostitutes are coerced in any meaningful way, and only about 10% of even *underage* prostitutes report having been coerced into the trade by any person (a number which has, incidentally, remained relatively stable since at least Edwardian times). And despite sensationalized claims to the contrary, only about 3.5% of all prostitutes in Western countries are below 18, and the majority of *those* are 17; the average age at which a so-called "child prostitute" enters the trade is 16, not the oft-cited 13 (*see page 45*). In other words, the fraction of all Western sex workers who could be described as "trafficked children" in even the loosest and least accurate sense is less than 0.3%. Criminalizing an entire type of human activity because of the exploitation of a tiny minority of those involved in it not only exacerbates the problem (see the paragraph above this one), it also sets an impossible precedent; if you consider it a valid response I suggest you learn to grow your own food, make all of your own clothes and chuck your iPhone in the bin (because if you sell it you are also profiting from exploitation).

The third, and perhaps most subtle, problem with this rhetoric is its philosophical bankruptcy and appeal to bigotry. The Australian activist Cheryl Overs has already expressed this much more effectively than I could:

> ...even in that overstudied "hotbed of sex trafficking" Cambodia, the only credible study [showed that] less than 2% of sex workers say they had been sold or coerced (CACHA 2008). How might this compare to the percentage of married women who were forced into marriage – even in the "hotbeds" of forced marriage? What percentage of gay men have been forced into sodomy? We don't know, but... it would be absurd to preface the words "bride" and "gay man" with "willing" or "consenting". Can you imagine reports that say that condoms should be distributed to "consenting homosexuals"? Can you think of anything more absurd, more homophobic or more stigmatising? Can you think of anything more absurd than describing Kate Middleton as a "willing bride"? Positioning "willing" and "unwilling" doesn't contribute to justice for people who have been raped, beaten [or] imprisoned in the course of either marriage [or] homosexuality and no one would suggest that. Nor would anyone suggest that rejecting the terms "willing brides" and "consenting homosexuals" amounts to a denial that those things happen. Yet this is exactly what the trafficking paradigm sets out for sex workers...

It is a sad fact of human existence that some people hurt and abuse others, sometimes for emotional reasons and sometimes for political or economic gain; it is also a fact that there is opportunity for coercion in virtually every human activity. The solution is not to retreat like frightened rabbits into dark warrens, nor to empower the state to police every human interaction in the vain hope that this will somehow help more people than it will harm; on the contrary, the solution is to *stop* trying to control everything and everybody, so the law is able to focus on those cases where one party has clearly wronged another. It is long past time for the blind guides of our society to stop expending so much effort in straining at gnats that they regularly swallow camels.

Circle

There would be no literature, no art, no music, no statesmanship if we relied on the prohibitionist for works of genius. – Clarence Darrow

I've written on a number of occasions about the origins of modern prohibitionist rhetoric in the second half of the 19th century, and explained how the "white slavery" panic (as "human trafficking" was called then) arose from a combination of racism, xenophobic fears of immigration, and the urge to impose Protestant Christian ideas of morality (including alcohol prohibition) on everyone. As I wrote in "Rooted in Racism" (*see page 179*), *"The First World War gave Europeans something real to worry about, but the panic continued in the United States until the Great Depression served the same function."* I thought it might be instructive to take a look at one of the larger prohibitionist organizations of the period, which at its height in the early '20s boasted over 4 million members, but fell to 30,000 by 1930. Its story not only demonstrates the mentality of prohibitionists, but presents cause for optimism in the way that this once-powerful movement fell rapidly into disrepute and eventually became nothing more than a marginalized group of social pariahs no reasonable person would want to be associated with.

The organization was founded in 1915, drawing its inspiration from a similar (but long defunct) one which operated for a while in the 1860s. Its members were overwhelmingly white Anglo-Saxon, Germanic and Scandinavian Protestants who felt great anxiety over increasing immigration from Eastern and Southern Europe, whose inhabitants they viewed as lazy and sexually depraved; they therefore wanted tighter immigration controls in general, but were especially concerned with protecting women and girls from rape and "white slavery". Indeed, most of the original founders were members of a group dedicated to demanding "justice" for Mary Phagan, a young woman who had been raped and murdered (allegedly by a Jewish businessman named Leo Frank). The group advertised itself as protector of the home and womanhood, and grew at an astonishing pace in the next five years, driven by sensationalized media coverage and reports that it had been endorsed by President Woodrow Wilson. Though chapters sprang up all over the US (and to a lesser extent Canada), it was primarily an urban movement which had its greatest political power in Indiana and its most rapid growth in Detroit, Dayton, Dallas and Atlanta.

All prohibitionist groups attempt to exercise social control by lobbying politicians to make more repressive laws, and encouraging more aggressive enforcement of existing laws. This one was no exception; it backed sympathetic politicians, assisted police in enforcing morality laws (just as the Hunt Alternatives Fund does today), and spied on violators of alcohol prohibition, then bullied cops into arresting them and courts into prosecuting them (just as "Big Sister" does to clients of Icelandic sex workers). It released propaganda to support its causes, and found a number of allies in the media who were willing to disseminate it via newspapers and radio. Many people joined the crusade due to this hype, and though a large proportion of them soon left when they discovered it wasn't to their liking, there were enough new recruits to replace those lost to attrition.

Eventually, though, the moral panic which energized the organization faded as all moral panics must; its members became increasingly desperate for attention and hungry for the power they felt slipping through their fingers. In 1927 some chapters began stepping outside the law to enforce their agenda, and the media rapidly turned against them. Newspaper editor Grover C. Hall wrote a Pulitzer Prize-winning series of editorials attacking the once-popular mass movement for what he called its "racial and religious intolerance"; other papers followed suit, and by 1930 it was all but gone. Not completely, though; in fact, it's managed to hold on to the present day, and still has about 6000 members. I'm sure most of you have even heard of it; its name is taken from the Greek word for "circle", *kuklos*. It's called the Ku Klux Klan.

The Rape Question

I claim that rape exists any time sexual intercourse occurs when it has not been initiated by the woman, out of her own genuine affection and desire. – Robin Morgan

At one time it was a subject rarely spoken of in public; now it sometimes seems that some people talk of little else. Since the 1970s rape has become one of the most politicized issues of our culture, despite sex being arguably the least appropriate topic for politics imaginable. The politicization of what could be considered the most personal of crimes began in 1970 with the publication of Carol Hanisch's second-wave feminist manifesto "The Personal is Political"; as I wrote in my essay "Politicizing the Personal",

> The only problem with [the essay] is, it's a load of crap; usually, the personal is just personal, and declaring it to be political merely holds the door open for increasingly tyrannical intrusion into people's private lives. The idea that "the personal is political" is borrowed from Marxist dogma and basically means that nearly any problem experienced by an individual woman is the result of "systematic oppression." If she's unhappy or has a screwed-up life it isn't because she's irrational, poor, uneducated, overly emotional, foolish or unlucky in the genetic lottery, or because she's made bad choices, or because the world is intrinsically unfair and many people of both sexes are unhappy and have screwed-up lives; it's because she is oppressed by the Patriarchy. This is, of course, a fundamentally defeatist, paranoid and narcissistic view which removes responsibility from the individual and places it into a social context that encourages permanent class

The Rape Question

warfare (or in this case, gender warfare). Since the two
sexes are different by nature and will always be unequal in
one way or another, this provided political feminists with a
path to political power; women were essentially told that
their situation was hopeless unless they supported the
schemes of the feminist leadership in its brave and
determined struggle against the Male Overlords.

Once one understands this, the reason rape was
politicized becomes obvious: Feminists could claim that rape
wasn't due to the criminal inclinations or lack of self-control
of individual men, but because of a supposed "rape culture"
which permeates society and encourages all men to rape and
all women to be reduced to an imbecilic state in which we
don't know when we've been raped until the feminist saviors
enlighten us. Had this notion been introduced full-blown in
1970 it would have been rejected as the rubbish it is, but it
came by slow stages. Remember, second-wave feminism
was at first a movement of strong, independent, educated
women; it was tied to the sexual revolution and its earliest
adherents recognized that sexual shame is one of the chief
ways in which patriarchal societies control women. The
miniskirt was a symbol of that freedom (hence the short
uniforms in the original *Star Trek*, which were a visual
demonstration of 23rd-century sexual equality), and sex
workers were active in a number of early feminist groups like
WHO (Whores, Housewives and Others, the "others" being
lesbians). So when feminist leaders wanted to call attention
to rape, they couldn't be wholly honest about it for fear that
women would stop being so sexually independent; they
therefore invented the myth that "rape is a crime of power,
not lust" so women would continue to put themselves in

danger. The fact is that old ladies who get raped are as anomalous as child prostitutes; the vast majority of rape victims are young, sexually attractive women in unsafe sexual situations. There's even evidence that conjugal visits reduce the rate of prison rape, and that legalization of prostitution reduces the rape rate.

The "rape is a crime of violence, not sex" mantra soon permeated Western society, and one could write an entire essay on the psychosocial reasons it did; in a nutshell, it's because the truth – that rape is a natural, though ugly, outgrowth of our sexual programming – is scary to men because it reduces them to the level of animals, and to women because it means there is *always* the risk of rape in heterosexual relations. By ignoring the 73% of all unwanted sex which isn't forcible (*see page 65*), people of both sexes could pretend there was no elephant in the parlor. But there were some people who didn't want that elephant ignored because its presence advanced their political agenda; just as first-wave feminism was eventually taken over by narcissistic middle-class white women, so it was with the second wave (*see "Feminists and Other Puritans" in Volume II*), and a cabal of angry feminists soon coalesced to lead those selfish, shortsighted women around by the nose. Since the "violence not sex" model no longer advanced their goals it needed to be replaced, but the propaganda campaign had been so successful it could not simply be tossed out; hence "rape culture", the dogma that neither men nor women could recognize rape when they saw it due to "cultural conditioning". In other words, an act both parties agreed was consensual sex might *really* be rape, not merely in a sort of academic sense but in a real *and prosecutable* sense.

The shift had already started in the '70s with radical feminists like Robin Morgan, whose wholly subjective "rape

The Rape Question

definition" forms this essay's epigram. That definition in one form or another spread through the feminist movement; not only did it conveniently eliminate the need for physical evidence, it also allowed anti-sex feminists to define sex work as "rape". But the weaponization of what was at first merely a farfetched radical axiom took some doing; as I explained in "Imaginary Crises":

> ...the FBI reported that 8% of all American women would suffer an attempted rape at some point in their lifetimes, and since only about a third of all attempted rapes are completed that just wasn't enough to create the necessary hysteria... [so] in 1982 Mary Koss of Kent State used... [Morgan's] definition to design a questionnaire she gave to 3000 coeds, and concluded that 15.4% of respondents had been raped and 12.1% were victims of attempted rape. But that wasn't the way the women saw it; only 27% of those she called "rape victims" agreed that they had...been raped, while 49% said the incidents were the result of "miscommunication," 14% called it "a crime but not rape," and 11% said they were not victimized at all. In true...feminist fashion Koss ignored the women's views of their own experiences and characterized their denial that they were raped (and the fact that 42% of them later voluntarily had sex with their "rapists") as evidence that they were "confused and sexually naïve" rather than that her theory was wrong. Koss' results were published in *Ms.* magazine in 1985 and quickly became gospel; the "rape" and "attempted rape" figures together added up to 27.5%, a fraction quickly abbreviated to "one in four" and endlessly repeated in pamphlets, articles, "rape prevention" and "sensitivity" classes and protest marches.

The Essential Maggie McNeill

Though the worst cultural excesses of early '90s feminism soon abated, it had already infiltrated academia and government and therefore became far more dangerous despite the fact that fewer women believed in it. Morgan's definition is one of the roots of "sex trafficking" hysteria (via the notion of all prostitution as rape), and as I explained at length in "Setting Women's Rights Back a Century", "...*the catechism being preached to young American women [is]: You are NEVER responsible for your own actions. No matter how irresponsibly you act, no matter what you say to or do with a man, if someone later convinces you that you were 'assaulted', or if 'authorities' rule that you were despite your protests, then you are a helpless, powerless victim without adult agency or volition, no better than an infant.*" In her 1991 essay "Rape and Modern Sex War", the ever-controversial Camille Paglia called for women to protect themselves from rape by being aware of its origin in male sexuality and avoiding situations in which it is likely to occur; Paglia's point, with which I wholeheartedly concur, is that "Women who do not understand rape cannot defend themselves against it." Naturally this precipitated a firestorm, and still triggers accusations of "victim blaming" whenever the idea reappears in any form. But there's a vast difference between blaming the victim in a forcible rape (as so often happens to this day) and holding women as much responsible for their actions while drunk in bed with an equally-drunk partner as we would hold them for their actions while drunk behind the wheel. And until Americans as a group recognize this, the culture wars over rape will be as endless as those over everything else involving sex, thus effectively drawing attention away from the real issues... which is exactly what those in power want.

Heroines

Power without self-control tears a girl to pieces. –
Wonder Woman, in *Sensation Comics* #19 (July 1943)

Regular readers of my blog or Twitter have probably
noticed that I like comic books. I don't mean romance
comics or Archie comic either; oh, no! I love superhero
comics, horror comics and science fiction comics of the
Silver (late '50s-early '60s) and Bronze ('70s) Ages. And
though I haven't purchased a new comic since 1980, I still
enjoy adding old ones to my collection or buying reprint
editions to fill in the gaps. I sometimes reread old issues, I
enjoy superhero movies and TV shows, and my strict
adherence to a personal moral code was inspired by the
similar moral codes of superheroes.

My affection for the genre began with two male
relatives; the first was my cousin Jeff, who taught me to
read. Since he was only three years older than I he can
probably be forgiven for quickly tiring of teaching me from
"baby books" and switching to comics instead; one of the
earliest ones I remember was a Superman annual full of crazy
Silver-Age "red kryptonite" stories (for those unfamiliar with
the mythos, this substance does not weaken Superman as
green kryptonite does but instead has unpredictable and
usually weird effects such as giving him amnesia or taking
away his powers). The other influence was my mother's
younger brother, who died of leukemia in his late teens just a
few months after I was born; he was made my godfather (a
purely sentimental gesture, since he was already terminal at
the time) and when I was old enough to understand I was
given a few of his things, including his comic books. Hence

my affection for the old sci-fi comics such as *Strange Adventures* and *Mystery in Space* which made up the bulk of his collection. And it was in the pages of the latter that I discovered one of my first heroines, Alanna of Ranagar.

Alanna was the beautiful daughter of Sardath, the most brilliant scientist of the city-state of Ranagar on the planet Rann, which orbited Alpha Centauri. Sardath invented the "zeta beam", a means of teleportation by which Adam Strange (a heroic young archeologist from Earth) travelled periodically to Rann, where he fought weird menaces with his intelligence, his courage and the invaluable help of Alanna, with whom he had fallen in love. She had inherited her father's formidable mind and was a scientist and adventurer in her own right, and Adam relied upon her wits and skills nearly as much as he relied upon his own. I was absolutely fascinated with the stories and wanted more than anything to grow up to be as beautiful and smart as Alanna, who (like John Carter's Dejah Thoris, Sherlock Holmes' Irene Adler and practically every woman in the works of Robert Heinlein) helped me to develop the mindset which later caused me to reject the false feminist duality of "a woman can be valued for beauty *or* brains but not both".

Nor was Alanna the only such heroine I discovered in comics; another was Shayera Hol, better known as Hawkgirl, who fought villains alongside her husband Hawkman as the first married couple in comics (that I ever heard of, anyway). Like Alanna, Shayera was beautiful, intelligent, brave, and a dedicated adventuring partner to her husband. Like Adam and Alanna, the Hawks showed me that the power of a well-matched man-woman team was hard to beat. The two ladies also shared something else in common: they both appeared in titles edited by the late, great Julius Schwartz, father of the Silver Age of comics and a former literary agent for such luminaries as Robert Bloch, Ray Bradbury, and H. P. Lovecraft. Schwartz loved strong women and was a supporter of women's rights at least since the 1940s; most of the ladies (whether heroine, love-interest or villainess) who appeared in the titles he helmed were interesting, well-developed characters who stood out in sharp relief against the flat, stereotyped females who appeared in most other comics of the time (such as the rightfully-mocked Silver Age version of Superman's girl friend Lois Lane, whose life was entirely dominated by schemes to trick the Man of Steel into marrying her). When I started selecting my own comics around my eighth birthday, I came to love another such heroine: Wonder Woman, whose adventures were overseen by Schwartz as of the July 1974 issue.

Wonder Woman was originally created by William Moulton Marston, the psychologist who invented the polygraph; he had previously written a book encouraging 1930s housewives to use their sexuality to help their husbands break bad habits such as drinking and gambling. Marston was a kind of male feminist; in 1942 he wrote:

> Wonder Woman is psychological propaganda for the new type of woman who should, I believe, rule the world. There isn't love enough in the male organism to run this planet peacefully. Woman's body contains twice as many love generating organs and endocrine mechanisms as the male. What woman lacks is the dominance or self assertive power to put over and enforce her love desires. I have given Wonder Woman this dominant force but have kept her loving, tender, maternal and feminine in every other way.

The Essential Maggie McNeill

As I discovered many years later to my delight, early Wonder Woman comics were chock-full of bondage and bisexuality; unfortunately, this type of content was quickly suppressed after her creator's death in 1947, and the character began a long, sad descent until by the mid-'60s she was nothing more than a joke. In the late '60s she was even de-powered and turned into an Emma Peel clone, and this sorry state of affairs might have persisted had not Gloria Steinem featured her on the cover of the very first issue of *Ms.* Magazine (July, 1972) and lamented her downfall in an editorial within. DC Comics took notice: her powers were immediately returned without explanation, and for a year (six issues) her title featured reprints with new artwork. Finally Schwartz, who was well-known for his own super-power of reviving failing titles (he had previously rescued Batman in 1964 and Superman in 1971), was recruited to fix the mess and managed to put the Amazon Princess back on track from the very first issue he edited. Luckily for me, the Schwartz Wonder Woman was really my first in-depth experience with the character; I previously knew her only from a single early '60s issue of my mother's and her appearance in the *Super Friends* cartoon show.

Though comics of that time could never have featured sex workers (except for one late '70s story I recall in which Batman got some information from a pretty streetwalker named Maria), I have no doubt that these heroines helped me along my path by teaching me from an early age that women could be strong without being bellicose, beautiful without being fragile and intelligent without being overbearing; that standing up for what's right isn't always easy; that it's a good thing to be who you are even if some others don't like it; and that a beautiful figure is nothing to be ashamed of.

Dirty Whores

Prostitution is pregnant with disease, a disease infecting not only the guilty but contaminating the innocent wife and child in the home with sickening certainty almost inconceivable; a disease to be feared as a leprous plague; a disease scattering misery broadcast, and leaving in its wake sterility, insanity, paralysis, and the blinded eyes of little babes, the twisted limbs of deformed children, degradation, physical rot and mental decay.
– *The Social Evil in Chicago* (1911)

In ancient times disease was usually viewed as a punishment from the gods; bacteria are, after all, invisible to the naked eye, and until the development of the germ theory the advent of illnesses seemed mysterious and even supernatural. The idea that disease is caused by invisibly-small organisms or "seeds" actually dates to Roman times, but because it could not be proven that such organisms existed until after the invention of the microscope in the 17thcentury, the theory was never universally accepted even in the medical community, much less among the general public. And even after Pasteur and others had proven the existence of pathogens, the notion of illness as a punishment for sin never wholly disappeared; rather, it merely mutated into a different form thanks to the realization that cleanliness (which, as the aphorism informs us, is next to godliness) tended to greatly reduce the risk of sickness. Those who led "clean", well-ordered, regimented and "godly" lives became ill much less often, and gossips might even explain an exception by whispering that the sufferer had deviated from "proper" behavior in some way. Since the popularization of the germ theory was contemporary with the "Social Purity" movement, the former neatly dovetailed with the latter in the minds of a large number of Britons and Americans and helped reinforce the push to outlaw "dirty" behaviors such as drinking, extramarital sex (especially paid sex), and even masturbation.

Even in ancient times whores recognized that certain diseases were more common among their number than in others, but these illnesses of the Classical Era seem to have been viewed as more of a nuisance than anything else; gonorrhea was completely unknown in Europe before the 11th century, and though lesions consistent with some forms of syphilis have been identified in Roman remains, the absence of any clear description of it in the medical literature supports the theory that this was a milder strain to which most people were resistant. As gonorrhea seems to have come back from the Middle East with the Crusaders, so syphilis seems to have returned to Europe with Columbus; though the "great pox" was well-established among Pre-Columbian inhabitants of the Americas, the first recorded European outbreak occurred among French troops in 1495, and they seem to have contracted it from Spanish mercenaries. This cannot be taken as evidence of rampant homosexuality in the French Army, however, because this early form of the disease was highly contagious even through casual contact and was both more virulent and far more lethal; fortunately Europeans soon developed an immunity to this "proto-syphilis", and by 1546 it had mutated into the venereal form known today.

By the mid-17th century European whores had largely figured out the visible signs of contagion, but unfortunately both syphilis and gonorrhea can sometimes be transmitted by asymptomatic individuals. So even though the rate of

Dirty Whores

infection among better-informed prostitutes was lower than among other promiscuous individuals (such as members of the upper classes), it was still higher than among the less-promiscuous middle classes, giving rise to the bourgeois notion of prostitutes as carriers of disease. By the early 19th century all but the least fortunate street workers were scrupulous about examining customers; in French brothels the madam herself generally performed the check before allowing a client access to any of her staff, and in English and American establishments the whores were quite as careful as modern girls, lacking only latex condoms as the final precaution. As one customer of a Storyville (*see page 195*) brothel wrote, "She approached and seized my genital organ in such a way as to determine whether or not I had the gonorrhea. She did this particular operation with more knowledge and skill than she did anything else before or after." But despite such published accounts and the research of medical doctors like William Acton (who despite his moral opposition to prostitution pointed out that whores were consistently healthier than other working-class women due to their precautions and relative affluence), the myth of the "diseased whore" grew; in 1864 the English Parliament passed the first of several Contagious Disease Acts, which were rationalized as measures to root out venereal disease in the armed forces but were actually nothing more than anti-prostitution laws.

The Act created a police "morals squad" which was empowered to define any woman in London as a "common prostitute", at which point she was arrested and hauled in chains before a magistrate who could order her to undergo a medical examination; if she refused (due to such minor details as, say, not actually being a prostitute) she could be confined to a "Lock Hospital" (basically a prison with a medical staff), forcibly examined and detained for up to 90 days, during which time the staff attempted to scare her out of sex work while "treating" her with mercury, a largely-ineffective "cure" which even many Victorian doctors opposed. Many were not sick when they arrived, but contracted other diseases (which of course were always interpreted as venereal) from the unsanitary conditions in which they were confined. If she survived the "cure", an unmarried woman so imprisoned would generally emerge to find her children had been sent to workhouses and her possessions sold to pay her rent. As if all this wasn't bad enough, a second Act in 1866 expanded the powers of police, forced prostitutes to register and condemned them to "health inspections" every two weeks; the third Act (in 1869) expanded the system to most of the country and inspired an NGO whose members "helped" the police by reporting any promiscuous or troublesome woman (or any woman who offended them) as a "prostitute", who was dragged away and registered no matter what she said in her own defense.

The Acts were so broad that they caught up huge numbers of unmarried working-class women in their dragnet, and so tyrannical that they even offended the sensibilities of many middle-class people. One of these, Josephine Butler, campaigned tirelessly against the Acts for 16 years, collecting a large following and eventually winning their repeal in 1886. Unfortunately, like so many "rescuers", Butler blamed prostitution itself (rather than society's attempts to suppress it) for the misfortunes of whores, and after her victory turned her efforts to the abolition of the profession. Her activism, and more importantly that of the sexually-repressed middle-class Christian female "purity crusaders" she inspired, resulted in the wave of prohibitionist laws which inundated Europe and North America for the next three decades; by 1918 prostitution was *de facto* or *de jure* illegal virtually everywhere in the Western world.

And though the tide of busybody regulation of individual sexual activity has largely receded in most of the civilized world, the United States remains submerged in it, and some things are the same now as they were in the 19[th]century. Busybody moralists still profess that their efforts to infantilize whores, rob us of agency, hunt us down, and destroy our livelihoods are "for our own good"; amateur women are still victimized by laws designed to "get" prostitutes; sex workers still face the prospect of our children being abducted and our goods pillaged by the State; crypto-moralists still believe that puritanical eating regimens and disinfection of everything are the keys to health; and the "dirty whore" stereotype is as popular as ever. Though the incidence of venereal disease is twice as high in the promiscuous segment of the general population as among street workers and only 3 to 5% of venereal disease in the United States is related to prostitution (compared to 35% from adolescents), the myth doggedly persists that whores spread disease. When one further considers that some studies have shown STD rates up to *80x higher* in survival sex workers than in those with greater resources, this means that the incidence of STDs in promiscuous amateurs is up to 160x that in escorts, and that escorts and brothel workers together account for only about 0.4% of the sexually transmitted disease in the United States. Yet every legalization regime includes mandatory (and often invasive) "health checks", while 95-97% of STDs are spread by the good, "clean" members of the general population who can legally screw anybody they like without even the most cursory or sporadic health checks, and face neither stigma nor revocation of their professional credentials should they turn up infected.

Bogeymen

I view the prostitute as one of the few women who is totally in control of her fate, totally in control of the realm of sex. The lesbian feminists tried to take control of female sexuality away from men — but the prostitute was doing that all along. – Camille Paglia

If I had to pick one single myth about whores which has done more damage to the cause of sex worker rights than any other, and which has inspired the greatest amount of wrongheaded, paternalistic legislation and the greatest number of dangerous, divisive, destructive policies, it would have to be the narrative that all or at least most women who do any kind of sex work (but *especially* prostitution) are dominated and controlled by violent "pimps". Long before "sex trafficking" hysteria inflated the pimp legend into a cultic belief, laws against brothels and "living on the avails" were based upon the fallacious but widespread notion that whores are somehow more vulnerable to male domination than any other women, despite the obvious fact that the typical whore has far more experience handling men and resisting their aggressions than the typical amateur. Like the Madonna/whore duality and the myth of the wanton, the "pimp" myth is rooted in male insecurity; self-doubting men have a deep and abiding need to believe that sex is not under female control, so they immerse themselves in a lurid, exciting and adolescent fantasy that female sexuality is always controlled by men (pimps and customers), and that all heterosexual women who are not owned by husbands are instead owned by "pimps" and "traffickers". Politicians who support "anti-pimp" and "anti-trafficking" laws thus cast themselves as white knights, "rescuing" helpless damsels from mustachioed villains who "exploit" them.

Female belief in the "pimp" myth comes from a similar direction: asexual or sexually immature women refuse to accept that other women might be so comfortable with sex that they can pragmatically employ it for income as one might employ any other skill, or might even actually enjoy it (with men even!) The idea that other women might be more sexually adept than they exacerbates their insecurities and must therefore be denied: the prohibitionist believes all women are as sexually stunted and unsatisfied as she is, therefore prostitutes must be forced into the trade by evil men (an idea which dovetails perfectly with the "male as oppressor" myth so beloved by radical feminists). The sex-hating female prohibitionist therefore becomes the ally of the "patriarchy" she so despises by supporting attempts to control female sexuality at gunpoint.

No matter what Western religions claim, sex is no different from any other human activity once the possibility of creating human life is removed by birth control. I strongly suspect that realization is the real driving force behind most of the current American anti-abortion, anti-birth control rhetoric: moralists (perhaps unconsciously) realize that without the threat of lifelong consequences, people will stop seeing sex as a magical sacrament which is "dangerous" without official sanctification. Without belief in the mystical significance of sex, prostitution is just another personal service like massage, hairdressing or wet-nursing; once one recognizes that one has to ask why feminists think it's "progressive" for a man to be supported by a woman if she's a politician or corporate executive, but "exploitative" if she's a sex worker. In "Thought Experiment" (*page 94*) I wrote,

> …the abusive, controlling pimp of legend is so rare we can consider him an anomaly. In fact, the fraction of prostitutes who have such an abusive pimp – roughly 2% – is so similar to the percentage of women who report that their husbands/ boyfriends are either "extremely violent" (1.2%) or "extremely controlling" (2.3%) that it's pointless to consider them a different phenomenon, especially when one considers that any non-client male found in the company of a whore will inevitably be labeled a "pimp" by cops or prohibitionists. The notion that hookers only have relationships with a certain kind of man, who is labeled a "pimp" by outsiders, derives from the Victorian fallacy (alas, still alive today) that we are somehow innately "different" from other women, and therefore our men are different as well. This is pure nonsense; the only consistent difference between the husbands of harlots and those of amateurs is that ours tend to be less hung up about sex.

The rest of that column presents an analogy between whores and barbers which may help you to see through to the truth of the matter. It's very important that people *do* understand, because the "pimp" myth is wielded like a bludgeon by prohibitionists. Claims of "exploitation" are used to demonize anyone who has anything to do with a whore, including clients, drivers, boyfriends, secretaries, landlords, dependent adult family members and even other whores working together for safety; a law in New York even targets taxi drivers who "knowingly" carry hookers in their cabs. The penalties for these "offenses" are usually greater than those for simple prostitution; the latter is generally a misdemeanor while "pandering" and "avails" charges are often felonies, and if the prosecutor decides to label such relationships "human trafficking" they can result in asset seizure, decades-long sentences and consignment to "sex offender" registries. Even minor criminal charges are then used by prohibitionists to label those so accused as "pimps" in a flagrant attempt to divide the sex work community against itself (*see page 192*).

It is precisely because of these concerns and many others that Amnesty International, Human Rights Watch, and many others who have studied sex work join sex worker organizations in recommending absolute decriminalization in every country, including the removal of laws which are represented as "anti-pimp" measures. As Cheryl Overs explained in a 2012 article,

> ...the [Global Commission on HIV and the Law] explicitly recommends that sex businesses are made legal, not just the sex worker. The Commission has recognised what all sex workers know – that laws against sex businesses mean they have to work in criminalised and therefore dangerous places. The spectre of the "pimp"...functions as a powerful barrier to supporting sex workers' calls for removal of all laws against adult sex work even among human rights NGOs and advocates. The reality is that sex workers in legal workplaces can challenge exploitation with the same tools that are available to other workers. This is fundamental to the notion that "sex work is work" and it is the embodied on the slogan "Only Rights Can Stop the Wrongs"...Creation of the category "willing sex worker" as a subset of "sex

worker"…suggests that very significant numbers of sex workers are enslaved, which is not borne out by experience or statistics. The risk is that programmes for health and human rights are seen as applicable only to a poorly defined subset of "willing" sex workers while sex workers deemed to be "unwilling" (or reluctant?) qualify only for raids, rehabilitation and anti-trafficking programmes. As I said in 2010 [*see page 58*], we don't talk about "willing brides" because forced marriage exists or "consenting homosexuals" because some men are raped…

A free society is based in the conviction that every adult person has the right to make his or her own decisions, even if others don't like those decisions or consider them foolish and/or self-destructive. Sex, whether or not one ascribes mystical qualities to it, is among the most personal of behaviors; it is therefore even less appropriate a realm for government interference than many others. Nobody but an individual has the right to decide which willing partners he will engage with, nor what their characteristics should be, nor how many at one time, nor how long the arrangement between them should last, nor why they choose to make that arrangement in the first place (*see page 139*). Because human beings are imperfect it is inevitable that most of us will choose unwisely some of the time, and some of us will choose unwisely most of the time. And when those individuals are authoritarian leaders, the consequences of their bad choices are not only suffered by themselves, but by whomever they choose to inflict them upon…or by those who just happen to get in the way.

The Privilege Paradigm

The war on privilege will never end. Its next great campaign will be against the privileges of the underprivileged. – H.L. Mencken

I finally figured out exactly what it is about the word "privilege" that annoys me so much. It isn't *just* that it's thrown about so often these days that its place in an identity politics or "feminist" drinking game or bingo-card parody would be a given; nor that it's often used (generally in the phrase "check your privilege") to shut down discourse; nor that it's increasingly employed by statists to subvert the concept of individual liberties; though of course all those things are part of it. In "Whorearchy" (*page 192*) I wrote…

> …I tend to tune out when sex worker activists start blathering about "privilege" as though it were some specific quality like height, skin color, IQ or income. There is no single quality in the modern world which confers "privilege" as birth once could, not even money or education. I'm not denying that some people are underprivileged and others start out with greater advantages, but this is inevitable in a world where everyone is different; even the *word* "privilege" plays into an authoritarian paradigm where there are no natural, inalienable rights, only "privileges" granted by beneficent "leaders"…Furthermore, early advantages no more ensure success than early disadvantages guarantee failure, and in fact a growing number of psychologists point out that too much privilege often makes a child (and the adult he becomes) fragile, maladjusted and less likely to succeed than one who has to struggle to achieve his goals…

The Essential Maggie McNeill

At the time, I knew that overuse of the word irritated me, but I couldn't quite put my finger on the exact reason. But now I realize what it is, and it's twofold. Firstly, a privilege is something that is conferred upon a person by others; we don't speak of a dog's "superhuman hearing privilege" or a bird's "flight privilege" because we all understand that these things are innate in the animal. Yet similar natural characteristics in humans are often referred to as "privileges", despite the fact that they cannot be considered such by any normal understanding of the word; no conscious entity "grants" a human a good brain, a healthy body or a stable neurochemistry, therefore these things can only be *advantages*, not "privileges". And that brings us to the second part of the problem: the word "privilege" implies an advantage which is *undeserved* and *unearned*, and thus something for which the individual so "gifted" supposedly owes some debt or obligation to someone else (generally God, country or "society"). The replacement of semantically-neutral words like "characteristic" with the semantically-loaded "privilege" is an overt attempt at emotional manipulation, an effort to make the fortunate feel guilty for characteristics over which they had no more control than their eye color or height.

Government's conversion of natural rights into granted "privileges" is a similar cognitive game; if civil liberties are unearned "privileges" magnanimously granted by beneficent governments, "authorities" arguably have the power to take them away again under certain conditions just as a landlord has the right to evict a tenant who has violated his lease. But when we recognize that self-ownership and personal agency are the birthrights of *every single sentient being*, governmental abrogation of those rights is seen for what it truly is: Violation. Usurpation. Theft. Rape. For example, the phrase "white privilege" pardons government for its systematic violations of the rights of minorities; if the way white people are preferentially treated in Western societies is a "privilege", an "extra" thing conferred upon some but not others, the onus of guilt seems to fall upon those who are fortunate enough to have received this "gift". But if we recognize the truth, that such treatment is the birthright of *everyone*, then the onus falls where it belongs: on those government actors who act independently or collectively to rob minorities of what is rightfully theirs by virtue of their humanity. Being harassed relatively less by cops, being treated more leniently by the courts and the like are not "privileges" conferred upon white people who otherwise would be treated as poorly as minorities; rather, minorities are cheated and robbed of their inalienable right to be treated as respectfully as white people. To refer to decent, respectful treatment as a "privilege" is to imply that *nobody* actually deserves it, when in reality *everybody* does. And nothing that rightfully belongs to everyone alike can reasonably be called a "privilege".

Against Conscience

Never do anything against conscience even if the state demands it. – Albert Einstein

So it has come to this: for a number of years now, it has been literally impossible to live in the United States (and a number of other Western countries) without breaking the

law on a regular basis; civil rights attorney Harvey
Silverglate estimates that the average American commits
three felonies every day. Nobody can pinpoint exactly when
the goal of universal criminality (*see page 188*), long sought
by the ruling class, was finally achieved; all we can say is
that it was sometime during the 20th century, an era which
opened with the criminalization of dozens of private,
consensual behaviors (ranging from non-marital sex to
intoxicant use) and closed with the "tough on crime" laws,
"drug war" escalation and discarding of the concept of
criminal intent in the 1990s. And though I will continue to
speak out against the government's granting itself new
excuses to abduct, torture, rob, cage and enslave people, the
fact of the matter is that it's several decades too late; any
enterprising prosecutor already has a wide variety of local,
state and federal recipes to choose from when deciding
exactly how he would like to cook any given goose.

A few years ago, Americans who like to imagine
themselves as "the political left" eschewed the traditional
label "liberal" in favor of the older term "progressive"; this is
especially interesting since the progressive philosophy
(which holds that the world should be ruled by experts who
are "scientifically" trained to know what's "best for society"
and therefore have the right to impose their will on everyone
else "for our own good") is if anything the *exact opposite* of
classical liberalism (which holds that each person has the
right to self-ownership and self-determination). In other
words, the shift in nomenclature revealed the truth previous
leaders tried to hide under the "liberal" label: the only
philosophical difference between the American political
parties lies in the fact that "conservatives" think the all-
powerful ruling elite should be made up of the wealthy and
religious authorities, while "progressives" think it should be

made up of those "educated" for the task in state-controlled systems. In practice, however, there is no difference at all. Both flavors of fascism favor infinite expansion of government power with the ultimate goal of total control of all wealth and every individual; both dole out bread and circuses so as to call attention away from what they're actually doing. And if you believe the process can be stopped by elections, legislation and all the other trappings of "democracy", ask yourself why each of the four presidents before Trump simply continued the policies of his predecessor even if his electoral platform stated the exact opposite, and why Congress is completely impotent to control powerful, entrenched bureaucracies like the TSA.

I don't pretend to know what the endgame for all this is going to be, but I can tell you one thing: it will be neither pretty nor peacefully-resolved. The American government is an immense, blind, idiotic hyper-organism which blasphemes and bubbles at the center of Washington amidst the thin monotonous whine of accursed flutes; it acts on instinct alone, and therefore cannot be counted upon to control itself even if its actions can clearly be recognized by rational beings as evil, chaotic and self-destructive. Because of this, no sane and moral person should accept any of those actions as having even the faintest trace of moral authority; in other words, the laws and regulations produced by the American political system no longer reflect sense, morality, the well-being of society, the will of the people or any other recognizable principle of good government, and are therefore not binding on free people. Police, prosecutors and other government actors who enforce such laws are not legitimate authorities, but rather the myriad tentacles of a mad, amorphous abomination flailing about wildly in its delirium and killing or maiming everything with which it comes into contact.

Given these facts, how is a moral person to act? The answer is, by one's own conscience. Any resemblance between the laws and moral behavior is now purely coincidental; this is not a problem for those of us who have always relied upon our own moral compasses rather than guidance from authority figures, but those whose personal senses of right and wrong have been stunted through reliance upon external dictates (*see page 110*) will be much slower to adapt. It's true that, as Voltaire said, "It's dangerous to be right when the government is wrong"; however, our government is so totally out of control that even following all the laws one knows of *to the letter* is no guarantee against destruction. The "law-abiding" citizen is a thing of the past, so it's better to do what one knows to be right even if it's illegal, because everyone is constantly in violation of some law anyhow. It's time for Americans (and all other subjects of repressive states, which means a large fraction of the world) to start practicing what Vaclav Havel called "living in truth": in other words ignoring the lies and proclamations of tyrants and just living like free people, avoiding all contact with government actors whenever possible. If you've never read Havel's essay "The Power of the Powerless", you really ought to; it's available in PDF form on the "Resources" page of my blog. Perhaps American fascism will eventually collapse just as Soviet communism did, but in the interim it needs to be thought of as something like a hurricane or earthquake: a mindless, super-powerful destructive force that cannot be controlled, but only avoided.

The Love-Hate Relationship

The prostitute is the scapegoat for everyone's sins, and few people care whether she is justly treated or not. Good people have spent thousands of pounds in efforts to reform her, poets have written about her, essayists and orators have made her the subject of some of their most striking rhetoric; perhaps no class of people has been so much abused, and alternatively sentimentalized over as prostitutes have been but one thing they have never yet had, and that is simple legal justice. – Alison Neilans

In "Heart of Gold" I discussed the "hooker with a heart of gold" stock character, and I mentioned that she has appeared in literature, especially Western literature, for centuries. But there is no doubt in my mind that she appears more often in American films and television programs than in those of all other countries combined (even if we allow for the larger volume of media from the US), and more often than not she is even allowed a happy ending. Given that (as discussed previously) such portrayals tend to indicate a positive or at least tolerant attitude toward sex workers, one might feel safe in stating that most Americans have a soft spot for whores. Yet at the same time, the US has the most oppressive, punitive, evil-minded laws against sex workers of any country outside the Muslim world, which would certainly lead one to conclude that most Americans hate whores with a passion. What's going on here? Is there some explanation for America's weird love/hate relationship with working girls? Yes, I think so; I believe it derives from the two separate and opposing, yet interlocked and seemingly inextricable, traditions upon which the United States was founded.

The vast spaces and distant location of the North American continent made it the ideal place for the displaced, disaffected and dissatisfied of Europe to go in search of their dreams. For some it was a place where they could build their own fortunes and own land they otherwise never could have; for others it was a place where they could practice their own brand of religion free from the state-imposed religions of Europe, and for some it was simply a place they could start over again. The key concept in all these dreams was of course Freedom (with a capital "F"), specifically freedom from monarchial tyranny. If there was ever a sacred concept in American thought, it would have to be Freedom. Of course, as with most sacred concepts, later generations tended to forget what the words actually *meant* (*see page 27*), but we'll come back to that later.

The practical capitalists sought the freedom to create wealth; most of them were highly educated gentlemen of the Enlightenment who were well-versed in history and philosophy and many of them saw the potential to create a Utopian state, free from religious or secular oppression, autocracy and the accumulated impedimenta of roughly 1300 years of European governmental tradition. So when they decided to throw off English rule and strike out on their own, their new government incorporated Roman-style checks and balances long since abandoned by European governments, but was otherwise based on the radically new theory of the social contract, the idea that governments were of and for the people rather than vice-versa. Though later abrogated and warped by power-hungry politicians in order to subvert its original philosophy, the American constitution was originally designed to keep the government from getting too large and consuming wealth as the Roman and later European governments had; it was intended to allow individual achievement while preventing the strong from preying on the weak. So from the very beginning there was a strong current of respect for individuality in the American character, coupled with an admiration for those who break the rules and do things their own way as the Founding Fathers had.

But at the same time, a vast number of the early settlers in the North American colonies were members of various religious sects which were unpopular in Europe. Some of these (such as the Quakers) were unpopular because they tended to disagree with kings a little too often, but most of the others were shunned because they were humorless party-poopers who were always preaching to everyone about what awful things fun and pleasure (especially sex) were. Modern Americans tend to whitewash and idealize the so-called "Pilgrim Fathers" who arrived on the Mayflower in 1620, but the fact of the matter is that they were a bunch of dour, prudish Bible-thumpers who would not be welcome at most modern Thanksgiving feasts. And though one might think at first glance that these sour-minded wet blankets would reject the pursuit of happiness so important to the Founding Fathers, one would be wrong; after all, it takes hard work, perseverance and sacrifice to make a fortune, and the Puritan Protestants were all about hard work and sacrifice. As these traditions met and interacted, the Protestant work ethic became inextricably bound up in the American Dream and the idea of wealth as a God-given reward for a pure and godly life became inextricably bound up in American Protestantism. And as the United States expanded westward, they became more and more intertwined until it was difficult to see where one started and the other left off. 19th-century notions of scientific and social progress soon joined the mixture, creating rich and fertile soil for the growth of the Social Purity movement imported from England in the second half of the century.

The whore is by her very nature a rebel who refuses to accept the conventional restrictions on female behavior laid down by traditional patriarchal cultures; as such, she has an undeniable appeal to a people whose entire nation was founded in rebellion against established order. Americans love rebels; though the North won the American Civil War, the struggle of the South against unbeatable odds was romanticized in American culture for about a century after the war's end (and still is in some areas), and outlaws such as Jesse James and D.B. Cooper still inspire folk following despite (or even because of) their crimes. Given that predilection and the fact that whores are the ultimate entrepreneurs, it should come as no surprise that many Americans tend to look kindly on us. I think this also explains the American fascination with streetwalkers in particular; the mythic streetwalker is a solitary figure who walks through the dirty, dangerous urban landscape in much the same way as the mythic cowboy rides alone through the dirty, dangerous landscape of the legendary Wild West. With her outrageous clothes and no-nonsense attitude, she makes as powerful a cinematic image as the cowboy does, and indeed her Western equivalent, the "soiled dove" or saloon girl, is often paired with the cowboy. This is, I think, the reason for the persistent tendency to imagine all whores as streetwalkers; when the average person thinks of us, the condensed image of a century of Hollywood streetwalkers strolls unbidden through his mind.

The Love-Hate Relationship

The other major root of the American character, however, lies buried deep in the cold and stony soil of New England, nourished by four hundred years of Puritan prudery and nursed by the likes of Cotton Mather and Jonathan Edwards. That aspect is not amused by the harlot, nor does it find her even slightly endearing. It finds our refusal to submit to male domination appalling, our refusal to obey every Biblical injunction shocking, our avoidance of "honest work" outrageous and our making a living from ess-ee-ecks completely unacceptable. "Fornication!" screams Mather; "Sin and Damnation!" screams Edwards, and this dark, dismal part of the American psyche is ready to drag the whore to the pillory, whip her soundly and brand her forevermore with a scarlet letter.

For the first century of the new nation, Lady Liberty and Uncle Sam argued and wrestled and struggled over their harlot daughters; this conflict generally resulted in our profession existing in a sort of twilight status, neither wholly legal nor strictly illegal. This was especially true in areas which were not quite mainstream America yet; prostitution thrived in places like New Orleans, San Francisco and the "wild" western territories which had not yet become permeated with the stink of Puritan repression. Alas, that all changed around the turn of the 20th century: the Civil War had established the pre-eminence of the federal government over those of the states; the now-huge country required an equally huge bureaucracy to run; mass communications and rapid steam transit made it possible to enforce Northeastern ideas of rigid, centralized government on the more freewheeling and independent populations of the Southern and Western states; and the Social Purity crusaders descended on the country like a plague of locusts, banning everything which carried a hint of decadence and "sin" about it. By 1918 prostitution was illegal everywhere in the United States, and with a few rare exceptions has remained so ever since. The average American has in recent decades dropped into a fearful sleep haunted by nightmares of terrorists, illegal aliens, "human traffickers", Satanists and "pedophiles" and he covers his head with a pillow and cries for Big Brother to protect him from the products of his own imagination. The cowboy has been "deconstructed" and the proud whore has been turned into a helpless victim, and the only places in which they retain their old status in the American mind are those shared fantasies we call movies and television shows.

The Dance of Death

You might be a king or a little street sweeper,
But sooner or later you dance with the Reaper.
– *Bill & Ted's Bogus Journey*

The Day of the Dead has been called by many names over the centuries (Samhain, All Hallows Day and *El Dia de los Muertos* are but a few), and it has been observed at a number of different points on the calendar, but that hardly matters: Death is the one great universal experience, the sacrament shared by every dynamic thing from the most ephemeral of microbes to the stars and galaxies themselves, the inescapable conclusion to every form of existence not already dead in its immutability. As such, the day on which we celebrate it is immaterial, though mid-autumn to me seems a properly symbolic time.

The Dance of Death

The irrational fear of death has increased dramatically as people have become less accustomed to it (due to both the decreasing violence of human life and the increasing disconnection of human existence from the natural world). Many live their entire lives in dread of it; they submit to any tyrant who falsely promises to delay it for a while, stunt and warp the development of their progeny in a foolish attempt to "protect" them from it, and deny themselves many of the pleasures of life, even to the point of restricting themselves to the consumption of life-forms they can pretend weren't validly alive in the first place. To these people the traditional depiction of Death, a terrifying figure who cuts down human lives like so much ripe wheat, is the most meaningful one; they see it as a monster, a pitiless destroyer to be fled for as long as possible no matter what the cost.

But this is not the only depiction of Death we find in the iconography of our species. Though its comparative distance from modern daily life has resulted in most developing a paralyzing dread of it, that same distance has allowed wiser heads a sense of perspective: in recent centuries some depictions of Thanatos have become more complex and nuanced, even positive. Now that it no longer stalks our lives as closely as it did for most of history, some have even begun to realize that a world without it would be cold and static: life and growth require change, and change must eventually lead to dissolution. A world without death would be one without development or advancement, a world as still and inert as an insect trapped in amber. And because this is *not* such a world, death can also be something else: a release. We have learned to prolong life, but often at the cost of sickness, torment and debility; all too often, modern medicine is nothing more than a cheat, denying to Death an organism which Life has abandoned. At such time, Death may become a longed-for companion, a lover who, after a long flirtation, one is at last eager to embrace.

Obviously, neither extreme is desirable for the majority of a human life; our species itself would be doomed if too many young people were overly enamored of the Ever-Smiling One, and we've already seen what happens when an entire culture hides under its collective bed and refuses to risk even the most casual encounter with It. The Dance of Life is, paradoxically, also a dance with Death; the steps are many and intricate, and we change partners many times as we move across the decades. And when the time for the final figure comes at last we should not make fools of ourselves with spastic capers in a vain attempt to change the pattern, but rather take the long-anticipated partner's hand and pass gracefully from the floor to make room for the new dancers who are always waiting for their turn.

Thought Experiment

The dignity of man is in free choice. – Max Frisch

One of the most important negative effects of the popular concept that sex is somehow magically different from all other behaviors is the modern fixation on pimps. The nightmares of anti-sex feminists and the masturbatory fantasies of trafficking fetishists teem with brutal (and usually dark-skinned) men (*see page 76*) who force women into prostitution, despite the fact that, as I've pointed out on numerous occasions, the abusive, controlling pimp of legend is so rare we can consider him an anomaly. In fact, the fraction of prostitutes who have such an abusive pimp – roughly 2% – is so similar to the percentage of women who report that their husbands/boyfriends are either "extremely violent" (1.2%) or "extremely controlling" (2.3%) that it's pointless to consider them a different phenomenon, especially when one considers that any non-client male found in the company of a whore will inevitably be labeled a "pimp" by cops or prohibitionists. The notion that whores only have relationships with a certain kind of man, who is labeled a "pimp" by outsiders, derives from the Victorian fallacy (alas, still alive today) that we are somehow innately "different" from other women, and therefore our men are different as well. This is pure nonsense; the only consistent difference between the husbands of amateurs and those of pros is that ours tend to be less hung up about sex.

Yet the myth, anchored as it is in prohibitionist mythology, male insecurity and Hollywood stereotypes, is a persistent and pernicious one, affecting even those who recognize that most prostitutes are in the trade voluntarily. A great deal of the milder trafficking rhetoric revolves around locating and identifying "sex slaves" and penetrating their supposed "brainwashing" in order to "rescue" them, and judges and prosecutors stumble all over themselves when endeavoring to come up with inane and tautological justifications for persecuting so-called "pimps" whom they concede were fair businessmen who worked to protect their girls. Even among many independent internet-based escorts there's a low-level hysteria about pimps (as though a man somehow has the power to reach through their cell phones and abduct them into a brothel overseas), and more than one reader has asked how he can avoid "pimped" girls.

At first, I answered such questions as they were asked, but eventually I realized that every time I did so I was feeding into the false dichotomy of "free" vs. "coerced" (*see page 145*). So eventually I decided to cut to the heart of the matter when a reader asked, *"Is there even a grain of truth in this trafficking stuff, some 'dark side' I haven't really seen despite my extensive experience? If this stuff DOES happen – how do guys who pay for sex make sure they're not contributing to hurting a woman this way?"*

For the most part, so-called "trafficking" is just people crossing borders to work (*see page 179*), sometimes without proper documentation but not always. This doesn't mean that every woman in every brothel is there because she wants to be and for no other reason, but does anyone believe that most women who work as hotel maids or grocery clerks are there out of free choice? Of course not, but neither were they abducted from their homes, carried off into bondage, threatened and all that jazz. Yes, there are a few examples of extreme coercion which are repeated endlessly by the fanatics, often exaggerated or with details omitted, and sometimes even rephrased so as to look like new ones. But in the overwhelming majority of cases, women do sex work for the same reason they do any other kind of work: because they need money. The number of women who are "coerced" into sex work is no higher than the number "coerced" into any other kind of work. If you're at Wal-Mart, how do you know your cashier doesn't have a lazy boyfriend at home who forces her to work and takes her money? *You don't.* And are you somehow wrong or immoral for checking your purchases out in her line if she does?

Thought Experiment

Let's imagine a barbershop which caters to a male clientele; they just do regular haircuts, nothing fancy, but all the barbers are female. Guys come in, get their hair cut, talk to the barbers, perhaps know their names. Maybe a guy even has a favorite girl who always cuts his hair; she does a good job, is friendly and she's nice to look at, too. But what does he really know about her? Only what she cares to tell him, and nothing more. He doesn't know what financial pressures she's under, how much high-interest debt she has, how psychologically stable she is, if she was sexually abused as a child, whether she's in the country legally, whether her boss treats her fairly and what her boyfriend is like. And you know what? None of that is any of his business unless she volunteers it; it's outside the bounds of polite business conversation. If his barber is under financial or emotional duress, is he somehow responsible? After all, men don't *need* to cut their hair; their demand for haircuts has created a market in which poor women are exploited to do work they may hate and possibly don't want to do.

What if his barber actually has a degree in philosophy from an expensive school which she incurred massive student-loan debt to obtain, and is under threat of arrest from the government if she defaults, but she can't get a job in this economy so she's struggling with a debt which at her current rate of repayment will literally *never* be discharged? Is she in "debt bondage", and is the federal government a "pimp" or "human trafficker" for telling her she needs to pay off her debt *or else*? If her parents cosigned those loans, the federal "traffickers" even keep her in line with threats to harm her family. And if a man gets a haircut from her, is he "enabling" that situation…or is he contributing toward her survival until she can find something which pays better?

Adult women are *adults*. It isn't the job of strangers, nor that of the government or of "rescue" organizations, to police their private lives. The essence of freedom, of individuality, of adulthood, is self-determination, and to deny a person that is to infantilize her. It's unfortunate that some people get into bad situations, often through no fault of their own. But unless the victim of such misfortune wants and asks for help, it is demeaning and abusive to force it upon her under the premise that her "rescuer" is better or smarter or wiser or more mature or saner than she is, and therefore more qualified to make decisions for her than she is for herself. Furthermore, it's both rude and arrogant for a stranger to presume he has the right to question her on her financial situation, reasons for working and conditions of her relationships with men. Nobody would behave in such a way toward a barber…so why do people think it's OK or even necessary to do it to a sex worker?

Ask yourself: Is sex degrading or dehumanizing? Is work? Is being paid? No? Then how can sex work be? Why doesn't the U.S. government prosecute Nike for its sweatshops in Southeast Asia or Apple for its sweatshops in China, and why aren't these countries placed on "watchlists" by the State Department for allowing them to exist? Why don't we see campaigns to "end demand" for sneakers or iPhones? Because they don't involve sex, and that is the *only* difference.

Objectification Overruled

No one can make you feel inferior without your consent.
– Eleanor Roosevelt

Feminists of nearly all stripes are always blathering about the "objectification" of women, as if society, the media, the magical "male gaze" or whatever had the power to *literally* transform women into inanimate objects like the aliens in a certain memorable episode of *Star Trek*. To any reasonable person, the very idea is absurd; women are not passive "things" and cannot be transformed into such by any process known to modern science, nor are humans machines to be programmed by "society" or "The Patriarchy" (or whatever other devil one cares to conjure) into treating other humans in any particular way. To be sure, the weak-minded are subject to considerable social pressure which colors their thinking about others, but only the completely brainwashed (who are and always have been a small minority) are wholly unable to see individuals as individual.

This is why the process of demonization works so well in maintaining hostility toward minority groups; the average person doesn't deal with members of any given minority nearly as often as with members of the majority, and if hate or fear toward that group can be maintained he isn't likely to have an intimate enough relationship with any of its members to learn that the prejudice and propaganda are false. If black people or Jews are segregated into ghettos and prohibited from frequent interaction with the majority, members of that majority don't get the opportunity to learn the truth about them; and if queers and whores are criminalized they are afraid to expose themselves to the

99

majority. But women are not a minority; we are, in fact, a slight majority, and it's a rare human who is not on intimate terms with at least one of us. Contrary to feminist propaganda, it is *impossible* to truly convince a majority of the population that women are something other than we are, because most of the population are women and the majority of the men are in the position to observe plenty of examples of individual female behavior.

The word "objectification" derives from the concept of a "sex object". But sexual desire is transitive; it *requires* an object. The word "object" in the phrase "sex object" is therefore used in the sense of "object of the preposition" or "object of one's affection", not in the sense of "inanimate object". Women *are* sex objects for heterosexual men, and anyone who doesn't like it needs to take it up with Nature (and find another way for us to reproduce). Furthermore, the human body *is* an object in the concrete sense; it's a physical thing which can be touched, takes up space, etc. Only the will or spirit animates it, and even then the body is merely a vehicle for the self. So I have a lot of trouble with people who decry the "objectification" of something which is already an object, in both senses of the word. I reckon what radical feminists are trying to get at is that men or "society" ignore women's personalities, but that is nonsense; the fabric of society is largely woven and maintained by women, and (outside of some extreme areas of BDSM) the personality of a female "sex object" is just as important to the average male observer as her body is, despite what some feminists would like to believe.

OK, so what about graphic art? Women are a popular subject for both male and female creators and beholders of visual imagery, and even moderate feminists often decry the "sexualized images" of women they perceive as increasingly

Objectification Overruled

common. But what is an image? It's a collection of tiny dots (electronic or paint) on a surface, which the human mind chooses to shape into something familiar. But the image is *not* the thing; this is what Magritte is telling us when he paints a pipe and labels it, "This is not a pipe". It isn't; it's a *picture* of a pipe. And images of women – whether in advertising, porn, "feminist" art, medical illustrations or paintings by Flemish masters – are just that, *images*. Any "message", sexual or otherwise, exists in the mind of the observer, and judging by some of the sexual "interpretations" I've heard applied by some feminists to pictures I see as innocuous, their minds are very dirty indeed (if not highly disturbed). I'm not trying to be difficult or facetious here, but rather to help you recognize that the "sexiness" of an image really is in the eye of the beholder. Would you be turned on by a photo of two dogs coupling? How about two monkeys? Two chimpanzees? Two really repulsive people? How about a poorly-drawn sketch of a nude woman? An artistic nude painting? A black-and-white photo of a nude woman wholly without sexual context? What if it was a nude man without an erection? A photo of a clothed man in some situation that appeals to a kink you don't share? Some modern fanatics want to keep people from taking photos of fully-clothed children in public for fear that pedophiles might masturbate to them, and overzealous Victorians supposedly draped the legs of tables to avoid arousing the easily-aroused.

What I'm getting at is, people tend to see in a picture whatever it is they're predisposed to see; I wouldn't call a picture of a cop beating a man "sexual", but an extremely sadistic or masochistic gay man with a uniform fetish might conceivably find it so. Pictures, like attitudes, are powerless to "objectify" women; that can only happen in the mind of individuals, and even then only in those who are predisposed to perceive such content everywhere they look.

The Pygmalion Fallacy

These aren't the droids you're looking for.
– Obi-Wan Kenobi (Alec Guinness) in *Star Wars*

I am blessed with a high degree of natural skepticism, and therefore see problems in prostitution-related news stories that most others fail to recognize. Take the 2012 article which launched the current "sex robot" obsession ("How Would Robotic Prostitutes Change the Sex Tourism Industry?" by Lauren Davis in io9, April 15th, 2012), for example; a number of activists linked or "tweeted" it, but nobody seemed to notice the glaring errors that rendered it…well, to be blunt, trash. The basic and highly flawed premise, which still runs through most "sex robot" articles, is that robot women could be competition for real ones to anyone outside a narrow segment of the population, roughly comparable in size to those who prefer animals to humans:

> Machines have already changed the face of manufacturing industries, but what happens when prostitutes find themselves replaced by robots? Will machines populate our brothels instead of flesh and blood people? Will the social stigma of paying for sex fade? And how will the availability of robotic sex partners impact countries whose economies depend, in part, on sex tourism? In their paper "Robots, men and sex tourism," which appears in the current issue of the journal *Futures*, Ian Yeoman and Michelle Mars of the

The Pygmalion Fallacy

University of Wellington's Victoria Management School
explore how robotic prostitutes could provide a solution to
many of the problems associated with the sex trade, namely
human trafficking and the spread of sexually transmitting
[*sic*] infections...

Right from the start, these "management experts"
demonstrate their shocking ignorance of events in their own
country. There's already a solution to "*many of the problems
associated with the sex trade*" that doesn't require the
invention of electric harlots; it's called "decriminalization".
As I've demonstrated countless times, most of the so-called
"associated problems" only exist due to regulation or
criminalization, and almost entirely vanish when people are
left alone. But the next portion of the article is even more
clueless; it imagines a robot sex club in the Amsterdam of
2050 and is based on this astonishingly stupid premise:

> ...The Yub-Yum is a unique bordello ...staffed not by
> humans but by androids. This situation came about due to
> an increase in human trafficking in the sex industry in the
> 2040s which was becoming unsustainable, combined with
> an increase in incurable STI's in the city especially HIV
> which over the last decade has mutated and is resistant to
> many vaccines and preventive medicines. Amsterdam's
> tourist industry is built on an image of sex and drugs...if the
> red light district were to close, it would have a detrimental
> effect on the city's brand and tourism industry, as it seemed
> unimaginable for the city not to have a sex industry...

If you've read this far, you already know "human
trafficking" is largely a false paradigm embraced by racists,
xenophobes and prohibitionists as an excuse to criminalize or

103

pathologize the normal international and intranational movement of migrants, many of whom work in informal sectors. In other words, it's mostly a "problem" of definition; when a government puts arbitrary restrictions on border crossings and/or defines certain kinds of work as illegal or illegitimate, people who cross borders or do those kinds of work (and those who assist them to do either) are automatically defined as "criminals" regardless of whether there is any exploitation or coercion involved. The only way for there to be an *"increase of human trafficking in the sex industry"* in any decade is for restrictions on migration and sex work to increase…which despite current trends is unlikely to continue for another generation. To understand the full absurdity of this scenario, remember that "human trafficking" is just the new name for the "white slavery" hysteria of 100 years ago; then imagine a science-fiction scenario written in 1912 postulating a brothel in Berlin of 1950 staffed by eugenically-bred whores developed in response to an explosion of white slavery and Salvarsan-resistant syphilis in the 1940s. But it gets worse:

> …The tourists who use the services of Yub-Yum are guaranteed a wonderful and thrilling experience, as all the androids are programmed to perform every service and satisfy every desire. All androids are made of bacteria resistant fibre and are flushed for human fluids, therefore guaranteeing no Sexual Transmitted Disease's [*sic*] are transferred between consumers. The impact of…[such] establishments in Amsterdam has transformed the sex industry alleviating all health and human trafficking problems. The only social issues [*sic*] surrounding the club is the resistance from human sex workers who say they can't compete on price and quality, therefore forcing many of them to close their shop windows…

104

The Pygmalion Fallacy

This ridiculous wanking fantasy is entirely dependent on not one but *two* hackneyed examples of prohibitionist propaganda. The first is of course the perennial myth that whores spread disease; as previously explained in "Dirty Whores" (*page 71*), STD rates in the developed world are as much as 160x higher in promiscuous amateurs as in escorts, and prostitution accounts for only 3-5% of all STIs. If these academics' totalitarian utopia was truly concerned about such diseases, it would have to outlaw all sexual activity between humans and install omnipresent surveillance to enforce that law. And there's a far cheaper and simpler means of preventing fluid transfer between humans than imaginary "*bacteria resistant fibre... flushed for human fluids*"; it's called a disposable condom, and it has the additional advantages of being both real and widely available.

The second myth is much more subtle, and you may not have caught it. Prohibitionists (especially those of the feminist ilk) are fond of characterizing men's interaction with whores as "use"; they constantly speak of hookers "selling their bodies" or clients "objectifying" us. But as every one of my readers who has ever participated on either side of the equation knows, this is pure bunk; the vast majority of men who hire escorts aren't just looking for warm holes, but rather interaction with real women. Yeoman and Mars imagine their mechanical sex dolls as "*programmed to perform every service and satisfy every desire*," but while the former might be accomplished the latter is a lot more than a few decades away. There is a vast gulf between successful mimicry of casual human interaction in an environment divorced from body language and other nonverbal cues (i.e. passing the Turing test), and a true human simulacrum indistinguishable from a woman in a sexual interlude; those who proclaim otherwise are in the same intellectual tradition as those who predicted flying cars and robot maids by the year 2000. It may be that centuries hence the erotic appeal of synthetic whores will exceed that of human ones, but nobody reading this will be alive to see it.

Furthermore, normal men don't want predictable, "plastic" interactions with women, and escorts with bland and uninteresting personalities are never as much in demand as those with complex, fascinating personalities. No artificial intelligence can be programmed to merely *simulate* the nuances of a personality; to pass that test it would need to be *endowed* with a personality, either by copying that of a human (as in my story "Ghost in the Machine" from *Ladies of the Night*) or by creating robot brains so complex and intricate they could develop their own personalities (like Rayna Kapec in the *Star Trek* episode "Requiem for Methuselah"). But here we encounter an ethical dilemma; namely, what is a soul? Or expressed less metaphysically, what constitutes sentience and individuality for purposes of determining self-ownership? Any gynoid whose physical form and simulated functions (sweat, tears, scent, epidermal responses, etc) were indistinguishable from those of a human woman, and whose personality was sufficiently unique and unpredictable to pass as that of a woman in the close interaction of a date, would also be sufficiently human to pass any test a court might devise for granting human rights, and would almost certainly be interested in obtaining such. Then we're right back where we started, except that the "trafficked slaves" would not be people mislabeled as such by moralists who disapproved of their choices, but sentient beings actually and wholly owned as chattel.

Vulnerability

The fashionable anti-sex work dogma of our times is that prostitution is "paid rape", an exertion of "patriarchal dominance" by violent men acting out their misogyny through the "buying" of women. The most fanatical of the True Believers proclaim that all sex workers are in reality "slaves" who are "owned" by pimps and traded like cattle, while those with a slightly less tenuous grasp on reality will (if pressed) admit that it actually isn't like that most of the time, but that we simply don't recognize our enslavement because we suffer from "false consciousness" as a result of the "social construction" of our sex roles under evil, evil Patriarchy. "End Demand" strategies, the Swedish model and "sex trafficking" hysteria all draw on this bizarre paradigm, which is an almost exact reversal of the typical harlot-client relationship; there is a vulnerable party in the transaction, all right, but it isn't the woman.

Because I insisted that my escort service advertising appeal to my own aesthetics, it was perhaps more "female-friendly" than that of some of the other agencies; as a result I attracted a disproportionate number of young, inexperienced applicants. And because the three other agencies with which I was friendly all knew that I was more maternal and patient than they were, they usually sent inexperienced girls to me as well. Many a time I sat on the couch with a young lady who was understandably nervous about going on a call for the first time, and asked how she should handle her fears; I replied that it was not really all that different from a blind date, and that after a week or so she would discover that the clients were often far more nervous than she was. I never once had a girl come back to me weeks later and say that I was wrong, and many took the time to tell me how right I had been.

A typical client faces just as many unknowns as a typical sex worker does. Even after phone or email conversation, neither knows what the other will really be like in person; either could intend to cheat or harm the other, and under criminalization either could be a cop. And while it's certainly true that the average man is much stronger than the average woman, many clients are elderly, infirm or in poor health; it's also not unknown for female thieves to pose as whores in order to entice men into private quarters so a male confederate can rob them. Furthermore, on average the client has a lot more to lose than the sex worker; while he is likely to be established and married with a reputation he does not want to lose, she is likely to be far less well-known in the community. And if she's done her screening properly, she knows his legal name and some personal information, while he knows only her stage name and (if he's done *his* screening properly) her professional reputation.

As if all that weren't enough, there's the familiarity factor; every person gets more comfortable with doing something through repetition. The more anyone goes into a similar situation the more they learn its ins and outs, its highs and lows, its likelihoods and its rarities; they develop instincts regarding it, can assess potential problems, and learn how to solve or escape those problems. But while a high-volume sex worker might see as many as ten or twenty clients per week, the typical regular client won't exceed ten or twenty dates per year; a hooker who's been on the job for a month has the equivalent experience of a client who's been hiring professionals for *years*. Experience leads to mastery and confidence, which increases self-esteem; sex work researcher Ron Weitzer found that over 72% of escorts report

Vulnerability

that their self-esteem increased after entering the trade. Clients, on the other hand, have to contend with demeaning or demonizing cultural messages about men who buy sex in addition to their doubts or fears about a comparatively less familiar transaction.

As any experienced escort could tell you, it shows. Many clients are as nervous as the proverbial long-tailed cat, sometimes to such a degree that they get cold feet and cancel (or merely fail to show up or answer the door). Others require "liquid courage", sometimes to the point that it impairs their performance; others insist on looking around for hidden pimps or asking questions intended to reveal police affiliation or (in the case of younger girls) legal age status. As a blogger I receive far more questions from men than women, and many of them reveal other fears and concerns: they worry about penis size, performance, unattractiveness or disease; about accidentally causing harm or contributing to exploitation; about ethics, guilt and the proper way to treat their escorts; and even about falling in love with a working girl. I remember one gent who was *so* nervous he angered several ladies by his vacillation, and sought my advice in overcoming it. To be sure, these men are not the majority; most clients seeing a particular escort for the first time are either a little shy or else no more unsure than a man going into any new business relationship. But the very nervous are a substantial minority, and vastly outnumber the abusive monsters on which prohibitionists are so firmly fixated.

The Suppression of Virtue

**Freedom, morality, and the human dignity of the
individual consists precisely in this; that he does good not
because he is forced to do so, but because he freely
conceives it, wants it, and loves it.** – Mikhail Bakunin

Though most modern people consider the duality of
good and evil to be a universal concept, nothing could be
farther from the truth. Since time immemorial there have
been concepts of right and wrong, but the idea that there
exists a morality untied to the pronouncements of leaders or
deities is a comparatively new one (and indeed, one that still
appears to lie beyond the understanding of most humans). In
ancient times (and for a majority of modern people) "right"
or "good" behavior is that which obeys the dicta of some
authority figure, however arbitrary or contradictory; for
example, in the Old Testament Yahweh often orders the
Hebrews to break his own commandments, yet that
obedience is viewed as virtuous (consider also the story of
Abraham, who would've obediently sacrificed his son had
Yahweh not countermanded the order at the last second). But
during the 2nd millennium BCE, some philosophers began to
recognize that there are universal principles of morality
which do not depend on laws, and that moral decision is a
matter of higher judgment rather than mere mechanistic
obedience.

But when personal ethics conflict with laws enforced
by violence, something has to give; what is a moral person to
do when the right action is prohibited by law or immoral
behavior demanded by it? Even if a person is so dedicated to
Good that he is willing to accept state-inflicted violence as
110

The Suppression of Virtue

the price of being a moral person in a deeply-flawed world, state-sponsored malefactors will inevitably prevent or undo his good actions as soon as they are discovered, possibly at great cost to those he cares about. Consider the classic villain trick of compelling the hero to evil actions via threat of grievous harm to someone he cares deeply about; the state uses this monstrous form of compulsion every day by threatening to abduct the children of those it wishes to intimidate and subjecting them to life-destroying abuse and neglect. Such forms of compulsion are by their very nature evil because they remove the capacity for free moral choice, thereby making good impossible. A computer, a lower animal which functions purely by instinct, or an inanimate object under the influence of natural laws is capable of neither good nor evil; morality requires free choice, and a sentient being robbed of that choice is reduced to the level of a mechanism or a vegetable. The act of compelling action therefore exists in the same moral realm as imprisonment, lobotomization or mutilation; it forcibly removes an intrinsic capacity of the sentient being without its consent.

In Gnostic theology, God created the universe in order to make a space where the angels could be away from Him so that they could have free will; the Divine Presence is so overwhelming that no creature can choose to do anything but obey when confronted by it. And even though Gnostics believed that action resulted in the creation of evil, it also brought goodness into existence because without choice there can be neither. An example of the inverse appears in the novel and film *A Clockwork Orange*: when the Ludovico Technique conditions the sadistic young criminal Alex against sex and violence, he becomes unable to defend himself from murderous attacks or sexually contact a consenting woman. He "ceases...to be a creature capable of moral choice"; he is neither good or evil, but merely a sort of organic robot (hence the title). All the government cares about is that he refrain from prohibited types of evil; the fact that he can't actually be good is immaterial (thus proving that politicians are far less wise than 1st-century philosophers). Modern tyrannies pretend that paternalistic laws coupled with harsh punishments make people "good", but this is nothing but a low-level, society-wide application of the Ludovico Technique, and those oppressed by it are robbed of moral choice. As Sheldon Richman wrote in "Is Virtue Possible Without Freedom?" (*Reason* magazine, June 3rd, 2012): *"social engineers think they need to deprive us of freedom in order to make us moral or in some way better...so they use the law to keep us from discriminating, gambling, eating allegedly fattening foods, taking drugs, smoking in restaurants, abstaining from helping others, leaving our seat belts unbuckled, you name it."* The article discusses "On Doing the Right Thing", a 1924 essay by anarchist philosopher Albert Nock, who was nevertheless thoroughly Victorian in his ideas about sex; he clearly held extramarital activity (including sex work) in the same low esteem he afforded to habitual drunkenness. But despite his personal aversion to "loose living", he specifically rejects the notion that morality can or should be compelled by law:

> ...I remember seeing recently a calculation that the poor American is staggering along under a burden of some two million laws; and obviously, where there are so many laws, it is hardly possible to conceive of any items of conduct escaping contact with one or more of them. Thus, the region where conduct is controlled by law so far encroaches upon the region of free choice and the region where conduct is

controlled by a sense of the Right Thing, that there is
precious little left of either...living in America is like
serving in the army; ninety per cent of conduct is prescribed
by law and the remaining ten per cent by the *esprit du
corps,* with the consequence that opportunity for free choice
in conduct is practically abolished...a civilisation organised
upon this absence of responsibility is pulpy and unsound.

...freedom seems to be the only condition under which any
kind of substantial moral fibre can be developed...we have
tried law, compulsion and authoritarianism of various kinds,
and the result is nothing to be proud of...in suggesting that
we try freedom, therefore, the anarchist and individualist has
a strictly practical aim...the production of a race of
responsible beings...our legalists and authoritarians...keep
insisting...[that] freedom [allows one] to drink oneself to
death. The anarchist grants this at once; but at the same
time he points out that it also means freedom to say..."I
never drink." It unquestionably means freedom to go on
without any code of morals at all; but it also means freedom
to rationalise, construct and adhere to a code of one's own.
The anarchist presses the point invariably overlooked, that
freedom to do the one without correlative freedom to do the
other is impossible; and that just here comes in the moral
education which legalism and authoritarianism, with their
denial of freedom, can never furnish...

Even if it were true that an authoritarian nanny-state
was a "safer" society (an assertion with which anyone to
whom a cop or prosecutor takes a dislike would disagree),
that still would not make it a *better* society. Moral progress
does not begin with authorities bringing stone tablets down
from mountains, but with individuals who are free to act
openly on their personal principles, thus providing a good

example to others. The more freedom a society allows, the more new ethical concepts enter the marketplace of ideas; the less freedom, the fewer. People learn by doing, not by being done for; unexercised muscles do not grow, but rather atrophy. And it is impossible to develop a moral sense without the opportunity to make free moral judgments whose consequences are those which result from the decision itself instead of those arbitrarily inflicted by the state.

Chauvinism

When we lose the right to be different, we lose the privilege to be free. – Charles Evans Hughes

Language changes over time; words come and go, and new words are used in place of older ones. One word which was common in my youth but has since declined sharply in popularity is "chauvinism", meaning "blind and fanatical devotion to something". A chauvinist is one who believes his own group, belief system or whatever is superior to all others and refuses to even consider the possibility that it is not so; usually, he is willing to use state violence to enforce his own views. So although we've devised a plethora of neologisms over the past several decades, usually ending in "-ism" or "-phobia" and often cumbersome, awkward or improperly derived, we actually don't need any of them because "chauvinism" covers the whole spectrum without having to add yet another term to the ever-growing list. Furthermore, the word correctly places the stress where it belongs, on the bigot rather than on those toward whom his bigotry is

114

directed, and thereby makes the behavior pattern far more obvious.

When one accepts at face value the excuses by which chauvinists justify their positions, the true connections between those actions may be obscured or even wholly invisible. But once attention is focused on the chauvinism itself rather than on its targets, the connections suddenly appear. Take, for example, the current moral panic over "human trafficking", a term so nebulously defined that it is nearly impossible to make any valid factual statements about it at all. Looking at the various phenomena to which the label is applied –exploitative labor, arranged marriage, unorthodox immigration, usury, surrogate motherhood, sex work, even attempted rape – it's difficult to understand how they're connected other than the fact that most of them involve sex, travel or both. Furthermore, sometimes things which clearly seem to fit the popular definition aren't called "trafficking" at all, especially when a government or large corporation is the "trafficker".

But if one stops listening to the claims of those who spread the hysteria, and instead looks for common factors, it soon boils down to chauvinism: every single one of the things called "trafficking" is a transgression against conventional middle-class white Western ideas of morality and propriety. Nobody is concerned about immigrants doing awful work that middle-class people don't want, so this is rarely labeled "trafficking" even when it clearly fits the standard definition; but because sex work offends both conservative Christian and anti-sex feminist notions about "proper" female behavior, it is labeled "trafficking" even when it clearly involves neither travel nor coercion. Once we recognize that Euro-American chauvinism has become widespread enough to maintain a xenophobic panic, one can also predict that other forms of institutionalized bigotry around issues of sex and travel should be popular right now, and indeed that is the case: In Europe we see persistent attempts to block migration and ban Muslim clothing; in the US we see assaults on abortion rights and mass deportations; censorship is on the rise in both. Superficially, these things may seem to be unrelated, but in actuality they are all motivated by exactly the same thing: the quest to purge from Western society everyone who is different from "us". Our persons, practices and ways of life are assumed to be superior to everyone else's, so obviously every nonconformity is a contaminant to be removed, by violence if necessary.

There is one exception, but it proves the rule. LGBT rights was for a very long time an uphill battle, especially in the pathologically-prudish United States. Yet in the past few years, opposition to the cause has quickly withered and died with astonishing speed...astonishing, that is, to anyone who fails to take chauvinism into account. If one insists that the cause of opposition to gay rights is "homophobia", in other words a *particular* aversion to homosexuals, the rapid turn of the tide makes no sense whatsoever. But when one realizes that the same hatred is dispensed to *anyone* who is outside the norm, the reason for the change becomes clear: same-sex marriage. While LGBT people were chanting "We're here, we're queer, get used to it", progress was achingly slow. But once they started to stress how little different they were from heterosexuals – "Look, we even want to get married and form families like you do, see?" – opposition to granting them rights rapidly dissolved. Once the majority came to see gay people as sufficiently "normal", their chauvinism was no longer an issue; the same can be said for European Muslims who adopt Western dress. The problem is not any *specific* form of bigotry against race, religion, sexuality or anything else; it's a *general* bigotry against anyone who is viewed as the "other". And that is why the chief purpose of my own blog is to demonstrate how typical sex workers actually are; once the majority realizes that we are not dangerous "outsiders" determined to bring down their culture, they will stop treating us like an infection to be eradicated or quarantined.

Don't Try This At Home

The word career is a divisive word. It's a word that divides the normal life from business or professional life.
– Grace Paley

I once saw an article on a study which found that members of couples can probably tell when their partners are faking orgasm; it bore the provocative title "Your Partner Knows When You're Faking". My immediate reaction? "I'm a professional, Honey; maybe yours know, but mine don't." But that little joke set off a train of thought: isn't it likely that one of the reasons so many women are anti-whore is that they're intimidated by our superior sexual skills? To be sure, not every whore is a virtuoso in the bedroom; some get by on looks alone, or cater to unusual fetishes, or have incredible charm, and some just excel at marketing. But by and large, the average pro has both a greater range of skills and is better at each than the average amateur. Part of the reason is that we get a lot more practice, and part is necessity: except as noted above, we *have* to be better at it because our livelihoods depend on it.

I don't think I'm saying anything controversial here; the sexual proficiency of harlots is not really in dispute. Male commenters on my blog have often praised the abilities of their favorites, and our prowess underlies the myths depicting us as enchantresses, succubae and vampires. Insecure men fear that we will control them thus, and insecure women fear that we will steal their husbands (presumably to add to our collections); the whole "pimp" and "sex slave" mythology derives from the need to deny the legendary sexual powers of whores by pretending that we're the pathetic, powerless victims of men (*see page 76*). Nor are those women with enough sense to know that hookers really aren't interested in their husbands wholly immune; many of them find the very *idea* that other women are better in bed than they are somewhat upsetting. Remember, society defines a woman by her sexuality to a far greater degree than it does a man: she is assigned to either the "Madonna" or "whore" category based upon it; selling sex is called "selling herself", as though sex constituted her entire being; and sexual violation is supposed to utterly destroy her soul and irremediably pollute her body. Nor is it only traditional "patriarchal" thought which elevates female sexuality thus; anti-sex feminists are simultaneously obsessed with it and defined by their rejection of it. So it's not surprising that many women would be intimidated by the knowledge that others are better in the sack than they are; on some level, they see whores as better *women* than they are, and must reject that painful concept by imagining us as the exact opposite (*see "Drawing Lines" in Volume II*).

118

Of course, this is all a load of nonsense. Sexual ability is a skill, no more or less valuable than many others; it isn't magical, earth-shaking or ego-defining. Some people have a natural talent for it, and others don't; some take the time to develop it, and others don't; some earn their bread by it, and others don't. Yes, I'm better at sex than most women; I'm also an above-average cook and (so I'm told) an excellent writer. My business skills, however, are not very good; my housekeeping skills are mediocre at best, and my musical ability is practically nonexistent. The fact that I possess the talents necessary to succeed as a professional sexual partner does not make me a better woman than someone who lacks those talents, but neither does it make me a worse one; each of us has her role to play, and society would have a lot fewer problems if each of us concentrated on her own rather than attempting to perform, critique or manage everyone else's.

Cleaning Toilets

The test of a vocation is the love of the drudgery it involves. – Logan Smith

When it comes to housework, everyone is different; though some people are either OK with all of it or hate all of it equally, most of us are OK with some tasks and despise others. For example, I've known people who will let the dishes pile up onto the counters before doing them, and others who whine if they don't get "help" doing the laundry.

Neither of those bothers me at all; in fact my attention to both of them might be considered by some to border on the obsessive. Though I have a dishwasher, I must wash every dish by hand before putting it in there, and it must be done before I go to bed; even if I'm about to drop from exhaustion, every dish must be washed and the dishwasher started or I won't be able to sleep. While preparing feasts, I wash dishes every time I get a break so as to keep the sink clear. And though laundry is only once per week, I have similarly-stringent procedures for it: all clothes are sorted by color and washed in a certain order determined partly by habit and partly by relative load size. Nobody else is allowed to interfere in the process, and previously-hidden dirty clothes dropped into the wrong color-pile after the process of washing starts are likely to result in the offending item being hurled at its owner, along with various terms of opprobrium.

But lest you think I'm some sort of paragon of domesticity, consider my bed-making (woefully inept when even attempted, which is rarely), dusting (hopelessly inadequate) and clutter management (the less said, the better); since I returned to full-time sex work and now live in my incall, all of these habits have changed to suit the circumstances, but if I were to retire again I'd go right back to the patterns. And of all the things which need to be done to make a living space livable, none of them are as awful to me as cleaning bathrooms, and no bathroom-cleaning chore is as repulsive as cleaning toilets. Part of my aversion is practical: the filth that needs to be removed from bathroom fixtures in general and toilets in particular is just nastier than that which needs to be removed from other rooms. But the worst part is a conditioned response: my early adolescence was plagued by week-long attacks of illness characterized by violent nausea, and to this very day the characteristic odor of

Cleaning Toilets

even a *clean* toilet turns my stomach; whenever I have to perform the horrid task, I get it done as quickly as possible for fear of being sickened by the power of suggestion.

And that's only my *own* toilet; the idea of having to scrub somebody else's – or horror of horrors, a public one – is so utterly revolting that I would do almost *anything* else to survive before taking a job that required it. To me, cleaning public toilets is the most degrading, demeaning job imaginable, and the irrational part of my mind tells me that a woman would have to be completely desperate, perhaps even forced or coerced, to do it. If I were the sort of fanatic who believes it's perfectly acceptable to force others to live according to my idiosyncratic feelings, I might even push for the profession of charwoman to be criminalized as intrinsically exploitative and degrading; in fact, I might even campaign for public bathrooms to be banned altogether on the grounds that as long as they exist, *somebody* will have to clean them. Oh, I know that some people say they don't find it any worse than any other paid work, or even that they prefer it to the other jobs available to them. But obviously, they can't be telling the truth if they disagree with me; because my ideas and feelings are the only right ones, anyone who says anything to the contrary is either lying or suffering from "false consciousness". They might even be in the employ of the powerful janitorial industry! Did you know that 300,000 children in the US are forced into a life of toilet-cleaning every year? And that their average age is 13? It's true! They have to clean 50 toilets an hour, and make $300,000 a year for their traffickers while they make nothing and have to sleep locked up in broom cupboards at night.

Of course, I'm not that kind of person. I realize that
everyone has different likes and dislikes, different aversions
and motivations, and different thresholds of disgust for
different activities; I even recognize that it's possible for
other people to be perfectly comfortable with a job I would
consider a form of torture, and vice-versa. But because many
people are either unable or unwilling to understand this, it's
important that we take away *everyone*'s ability to inflict their
own skewed *weltanschauung* upon others, by eliminating all
laws against consensual acts; though it's impossible to make
all people tolerant and accepting of differences, we can at
least eradicate the processes by which fanatics force all of
society to pretend that their own subjective feelings about
various behaviors have some basis in objective reality.

Ulro

Now I a fourfold vision see,
And a fourfold vision is given to me:
'Tis fourfold in my supreme delight
And threefold in soft Beulah's night
And twofold always, may God us keep
From single vision and Newton's sleep! – William Blake

William Blake constructed an elaborate artificial
mythology full of original concepts, gods, places and terms.
One of these concepts is *Ulro*, an utterly fallen state
divorced from all abstraction and transcendence; he imagined
four states of being, with Eternity (also called Eden) being
the highest and Ulro being the lowest. Beings in Ulro have
"single vision"; they see only mundane physical reality

uncolored by imagination, inspiration or even fully developed eroticism. Ulro is the state occupied by the dullest sort of human, who is unable to see any of the complexities of the world around them; it is a kind of spiritual sleep, dominated by the stomach and intestines, and people who exist this way can be visualized as going through the world with one eye closed, seeing everything flat and without proper perspective. The second state, Generation, is the one in which more intellectually and spiritually aware humans exist; it is dominated by the genitals and can be imagined as seeing with both eyes. The third state, Beulah, occurs when the individual is open to the spiritual or imaginative dimension; it is dominated by the heart and characterized by "threefold vision", which one might think of as the "third eye" of mysticism, the "altered consciousness" experienced by psychedelic drug users, an ecstatic religious state or even a transcendent erotic experience. Finally, Eternity, dominated by the head and characterized by "fourfold vision", allows connection to the entire universe; it is a condition of total bliss which few humans can reach, and even then only for very short periods of time while existing in this plane.

I've been fascinated by Blake's mysticism ever since I first studied it while working on my bachelor's degree in English; my major concentration was on the Romantic Period, and Blake was the subject of at least one major term paper and a number of lesser ones. I wove many of his concepts into the D&D universe I created, and I often find myself looking at the world through a Blakean lens, especially when thinking about the incredible, half-blind ignorance with which so many people view the

The Essential Maggie McNeill

world, *especially* when the topic is sex. Traditional religions, authoritarian governments, power-hungry collective entities and the popular media all work – separately and in conjunction – to immerse the population in a dense fog of obfuscation, a Veil of Ulro which allows them to be just awake enough to serve their masters, but not awake enough to actually penetrate that fog and see the world around them as it is. They believe in the most ridiculous nonsense about sex, imagining men to be such eunuchs that they can simply be ordered to be celibate by churches, military officials, prison officials or prudish wives, and women to be so asexual that the only possible reason they might engage in pragmatic sex is because some evil man forced them to. They are "shocked" when government actors behave exactly like other men would under the same conditions, and refuse to understand that interesting costumes don't magically make men into paragons, but rather make them much worse. They actually think that the leaders *they* have chosen to follow are better and more noble than those on the evil Other Team, and obediently close their one open eye whenever those leaders order them to ignore spying, brutality, looting, racism, and even mass murder. And they're willing to believe in grandiose fantasies utterly divorced from all known facts about statistics, economics, psychology, sexuality, anthropology and plain common sense rather than accept that some women can have pragmatic sex, that most men are willing to pay them for it, and that many people are happy to strive for truly Pinocchian levels of dishonesty in order to make a profit, seize power, get rid of people they're bigoted against or even seek petty vengeance. Even Blake himself only claimed to have fourfold vision in moments of "supreme delight", and most of us need drugs, meditation or superlative sexual experiences to get our "third eyes" open.

Ulro

But is it really too much to ask that people just wake the hell up and open the second eye that's waiting and ready right there on the fronts of their heads?

The Girls from Tarzana

...in this splendid novel...Mr. Burroughs has...given you as remarkable a heroine as you might expect. For the Girl was a member of "the oldest profession in the world," and the hero was foreman of the grand jury. –
Editorial foreword to *The Girl from Farris's*

When I first encountered mentions of the Ouled Nail, an Algerian tribe among whom prostitution was common and accepted, I was excited not only because I found them fascinating enough to write about twice (*see "The Ouled Nail" and "The Angels of Dien Bien Phu" in Volume II*), but also because I had encountered the term "Ouled Nail" before. Regular readers have probably noticed that I have an exceptional memory, and can often recall unusual words encountered years before. And I remembered exactly where I had seen this one: in *The Return of Tarzan*, the ape-man escapes his enemies with the assistance of an Ouled Nail. In the book, the term is used synonymously with "dancing girl", and I was thrilled to discover the extra dimension which linked this character to my own profession. But Tarzan's friend is not the only harlot to appear in his creator's *oeuvre*, and the way in which Edgar Rice Burroughs portrays them in his work says a great deal about both the man himself and the early-20th-century society in which his stories were first published. If you intend to read the works (and I'd love it if you did), please be warned that this essay contains spoilers. Also note that *The Return of Tarzan* and *The Gods of Mars* are sequels to *Tarzan of the Apes* and *A Princess of Mars*, respectively.

As I've said before, when my beloved cousin Jeff taught me to read he preferred to use his own favorites rather than "baby books" (*see page 67*), and the authors to whom he introduced me over the next few years are still among my favorites. One of these was Burroughs, who is most famous as the creator of Tarzan but also wrote several other series and many stand-alone works in a career which stretched from 1912 to his death in 1950. Burroughs is generally considered a "men's author", and that is a shame because his books are full of romance and strong, interesting female characters; I honestly believe that one of the reasons I found traditional romance novels boring was that in Burroughs' stories I found love intertwined with adventure in settings which excited my young imagination. And though he was in many ways a product of the Victorian Era (born 1875), he had some very liberal views about nudity and sex which, though restrained in his earlier works by commercial necessity, are much more obvious in his writings of the '30s and '40s.

While researching "The Ouled Nail" I revisited *The Return of Tarzan* and discovered that, though Burroughs' understanding of the Ouled Nail is clearly faulty, he does hint at their prostitution in a passage from chapter 7: *"The frightened Ouled-Nails were crouching at the tops of the stairs which led to their respective rooms, the only light in the courtyard coming from the sickly candles which each girl had stuck with its own grease to the woodwork of her door-frame, the better to display her charms to those who might*

The Girls from Tarzana

happen to traverse the dark enclosure." The story takes place in 1910, after the French authorities had restricted the Nailiyat to working for licensed cafes, and the girl who tips Tarzan off to the planned attack and helps him to escape his pursuers is depicted as a slave, abducted by marauders and sold to the café owner. She senses Tarzan's nobility by the way he speaks to her and the respectful manner in which he tips her after her dance, and so alerts him to his danger at great risk to herself. Of course Tarzan rescues her from the café and returns her to her father, and in chapter 10 she again risks her life to rescue him from another band of nomads hired by the villainous Nikolas Rokoff to accomplish what two previous groups of hirelings had failed to do. Not all of the whores Tarzan encounters are so principled; in chapter 3 of the same book, Rokoff hires a Parisian streetwalker to lure Tarzan into an ambush by calling for help, and after he defeats his assailants she lies to the police, telling them that the ruffians had tried to save her from an attempted rape by Tarzan.

Burroughs also tried his hand at contemporary drama; the heroine of *The Efficiency Expert* (1921) is a prostitute called "Little Eva" who befriends the hero when he works for a while as a waiter at a cabaret she frequents. Her belief in him inspires him to apply for the titular position, and her unflagging support keeps him going when he is later accused of murder; he is acquitted due largely to evidence she collects herself, and only her death in an influenza epidemic keeps him from marrying her. I've never quite forgiven Burroughs for the poor girl's fate, though I'm sure he could not have used the ending I wanted in an *Argosy* title of that time. He visited a similar doom upon Daisy Juke, high-school

sweetheart of Johnny Lafitte, the protagonist of *Pirate Blood*
(written 1932, but unpublished until after the author's death):
after her family strikes it rich on oil, Daisy turns to drink,
becomes a high-priced whore in Singapore, and then the
consort of a powerful pirate; she commits suicide when
Lafitte discovers her "fall from grace". June Lathrop, the
heroine of *The Girl from Farris's* (1920) dodges the censors
in a different way; though in the first scene she escapes from
a brothel and we assume throughout the novella that she is a
(reformed) prostitute, it is revealed at the end that she was
actually the victim of a bigamist who had merely housed her
in a room rented from the brothel owner. Thus, she is free to
marry the hero without provoking outrage in the readership.

Burroughs pushed the envelope a little farther in *The
Girl from Hollywood* (1922), whose titular character,
Shannon Burke, is an actress who becomes the kept woman
of a director who "auditions" her on the "casting couch" and
then gets her addicted to morphine in order to control her.
While shooting on location at the Rancho del Ganado (a
fictionalized version of Burroughs' own Tarzana ranch, on
which the town of Tarzana, California was later built) she
befriends the Pennington family (based on the Burroughs
family), who help her to break her addiction and even forgive
her for her sordid past. The standards of the day did not
allow Burroughs to allow an unrepentant whore a happy
ending, and indeed the two heroines who are specifically
described as prostitutes (and not excused via enslavement or
downplayed as kept women) have to be killed off at the end
as in *Camille*. However, I think it's clear that in all of these
cases he does his best to show that the mere fact of a "sinful"
life does not make a woman "bad", and indeed his fictional
analog even bestows his blessings on a relationship between
such a woman and his own fictional son!

The Girls from Tarzana

My final example (and certainly the most coy treatment of the subject) is Thuvia, Princess of Ptarth on the planet Mars. Burroughs' Martians believe in a physical paradise at the South Pole of their planet, presided over by a race of living gods called the Therns; those who are very old (their natural lifespan is over a thousand years) or tired of life can make a Pilgrimage to this paradise and never return to the outer world. But as the hero John Carter discovers in *The Gods of Mars* (1913), the whole thing is a gigantic hoax perpetrated by the evil and cannibalistic Therns, and those who make the Pilgrimage are captured and either eaten or enslaved. Some years before Carter's arrival, the beautiful but moody young Thuvia makes the Pilgrimage (for reasons never disclosed) and becomes the plaything of a Thern leader. After her rescue by John Carter (who exposes the whole horrible scam to the world) she returns home and is treated like a virgin despite the fact that after years as the slave of a degenerate cult she absolutely could not be in any literal sense. The only thing I can guess is that, though Martian standards of female chastity are Victorian in their rigidity, an exception is made for rape; and though most Martian noblewomen would rather commit suicide than submit to violation, Thuvia instead chose to live. This is but one of the enigmas surrounding Thuvia, who is certainly one of the most interesting characters in the series; I believe her to be, like the Ouled Nail of Sidi Aissa, one of the earliest examples in the development of Burroughs' recognition that there was something not quite right in the conventional ideas of female sexual morality prevalent in his time.

Amazingly Stupid Statements

It is better to keep your mouth closed and let people think you are a fool than to open it and remove all doubt. –
Mark Twain

Though I suppose I should be used to it after all these years, I am still astonished by the incredibly stupid statements which are habitually made by prohibitionists. Everyone makes stupid statements from time to time (and I'm by no means an exception), but those who want state control of consensual sex doggedly and vociferously repeat the same asinine arguments over and over again, as though they were completely unaware of how ridiculous they sound. Anyone's brain can slip out of gear for long enough to make an embarrassing declaration, but the whore-burning crowd's constant repetition of these same idiotic assertions indicates that they honestly feel them to be both valid and persuasive. Let's look at a few of them, in no particular order.

The act of exchanging money for sex is inherently degrading.

Why? What portion of the act generates the degradation? Is it the act of having sex with men at all? Because if that's the case you had best just shut up now before somebody points out that you're naked. Or is it the act of having sex with people to whom one is not married, in which case why aren't you out promoting criminalization of infidelity, singles bars, gay bars and swinger clubs, or advocating for "abstinence-only" sex education? Or perhaps you believe that any personal service for pay should be
130

illegal, in which case where's all your anger and bile against masseuses, hairdressers, manicurists, physical therapists and cosmetologists? Perhaps you believe that stay-at-home wives need to be protected by prohibiting anyone from providing traditional wifely services for pay; good plan! So when do you start your campaign to criminalize chefs, tailors, nannies, maids and day care centers? No? It must just be that you're against the free market, then; good luck selling that one, considering that even the Russians and Chinese have embraced it.

Because *you* are too romantic, shy, introverted, conventional, prissy, prudish, narcissistic, lazy, fearful or misandrous to sell sexual services, why does that mean I can't? I have too much sense to believe I can get all of my moral answers from a 3000 year old book and too much decency to promote warfare between large groups of society so as to give me a chance to grab power, but you don't see me trying to prohibit you from doing those things.

Prostitution is unacceptably dangerous to women.

Who determines what level of danger is unacceptable, *you*? Who decided that an adult woman who can drive, vote, drink alcohol, own a firearm, see X-rated movies, enter into binding legal contracts and even run for political office is somehow incompetent to determine whom she wants to have sex with and on what terms? And having decided that I was incompetent, who the hell declared *you* my legal guardian? What other activities carry an "unacceptable" level of risk? How about joining the military? Construction work? Driving? Walking on public streets without a male escort?

Going outside without *niqab* and *chador*, thus risking rape due to male lust? What country are you from again? And since you're so concerned about sex workers' safety, can you please explain why you think the best way to help us is to make our jobs *more* dangerous?

No little girl dreams of growing up to be a prostitute.

Despite its deep idiocy, this one has actually become *more* popular since I wrote the original version of this essay in 2010. Assuming for a moment that by "little girl" you *actually* mean one old enough to comprehend what a whore does for a living, you're still wrong; I had a secret admiration for prostitutes from my early teens and the only reason I didn't embrace the idea wholeheartedly was due to brainwashing that an intellectual career was somehow "better" than one as an entertainer. Many of my friends and other sex workers I've talked to had similar experiences, and lots of teenage girls dream of being actresses or singers, who are nothing but glorified whores who make a living with the same body parts as we do; if our trade were not illegal and suppressed who knows how many girls might indeed want to be hookers?

But even that isn't the point. No little girl dreams of growing up to be a sales clerk, cashier, middle manager, real estate agent or maid either, so should we ban those jobs? And do you honestly imagine little boys dream of growing up to be accountants, insurance salesmen, bus drivers, coal miners and pipefitters? If everyone grew up to be what he or she wanted to be in childhood we would have a workforce made up almost entirely of firemen, ballerinas, astronauts, teachers, cowboys and nurses.

Amazingly Stupid Statements

Nine out of ten prostitutes would leave the trade if they could.

I totally believe this, but so would nine out of ten accountants, lawyers, doctors, secretaries, shopkeepers, clerks, waitresses, teachers, farmers, plumbers, cubicle workers, factory workers, etc, etc, etc, etc *ad nauseum*; in fact, for some of those I'm sure it's more like ninety-nine out of a hundred. There's a reason people get *paid* to do work, you know; it's an incentive to get them to do something they wouldn't freaking do if they were independently freaking wealthy! Those of us who didn't have the good fortune to inherit large portions of major corporations do indeed have to spend large portions of our time doing things we would rather not do with people we might not otherwise care to be around. But as I said two sections up, if you're so concerned about the difficulty of our jobs, why are you so dedicated to making them even *more* difficult?

X% (insert arbitrary & unsupported large number here) of prostitutes are coerced (or abused, or addicted, or "trafficked", or underage, or whatever).

I'm not even going to comment on the arbitrary nature of these numbers because it should be pretty obvious to anyone with half a brain that it's impossible to make any reasonable estimate of what percentage of practitioners of a repressed and largely-invisible group are blonde, poor, left-handed, green-eyed, uneducated, diabetic or anything else. The important thing is that even if some percentage of any given profession is affected by a condition which removes free choice or invalidates judgment, what the hell does that have to do with those who are not so affected? 85% of cops have anger management problems, sadistic impulses or self-esteem issues; 72% of lawyers are addicted to cocaine; 99.9% of politicians are moral imbeciles; 54% of doctors are only in it for the money; 95% of agricultural workers live below the poverty line; 113% of feminists are certifiably bat-shit crazy and 92.35% of statistics are made up on the spot, so why don't you go pick on them for a change and just leave us to the Bible Beaters?

Prostitution is a manifestation of patriarchal dominance over women.

Wow, really? Then how come we were respected priestesses in the old goddess-centered cultures, and our status slowly declined in the patriarchal ones? And why is it that (at least until the invention of feminism) the most patriarchal cultures are those in which prostitutes are most brutally repressed? If the "patriarchy" likes prostitution so damned much, why the hell isn't it universally legal in this world supposedly controlled by said "patriarchy"? This argument is as ludicrous as the feminist claim that sexy clothes are symptomatic of "sexist oppression" despite the obvious fact that oppressive, rigidly patriarchal cultures invariably force women to cover up *more* in public.

Prostitutes are anti-feminist because they earn a living by being subservient to men.

Anyone who has ever actually done sex work herself, hired one of us or observed the transaction will recognize this as easily the most idiotic statement in this essay. The male client is required to essentially beg and bribe a sex worker by jumping through whatever hoops she declares he must and paying her whatever fee she demands, however absurd and unfair; if he displeases her beyond the point she is willing to tolerate she may simply cut him off and leave, and he has little recourse other than physical violence (to which normal men are not willing to resort). Prostitution is evidence of one gender's sexual dominance over the other, all right, but it's the opposite way around from the sick fantasies of anti-sex feminists (*see page 107*); why do you think maladjusted men hate us so consistently? It's because our very existence is a constant reminder of the male sexual dependence on women (and our ability to manipulate men to get what we want by means of that dependence) that bitter men are so obsessed with controlling or eradicating us and sociopathic men so often murder us.

Perhaps academic feminists, few of whom have ever had to achieve anything resembling real-world results in order to earn their pay, intentionally confuse "subservience" with the normal necessity of any service provider to please their customers? If a female barber was rude to her male customers and did a bad job cutting their hair, she wouldn't last too long in her profession. Not even academic feminists are so addle-brained as to pretend that other female service professionals are "anti-feminist" merely because of the way in which they earn their living; that distinction is reserved for whores. Like every other example in this essay, this last stupid statement can more truthfully summed up in one phrase: "It's different because it involves sex."

Honored in the Breach

But to my mind, though I am native here
And to the manner born, it is a custom
More honored in the breach than the observance. –
William Shakespeare, *Hamlet* (I, iv)

      By the time Election Day rolls around in the United States, we've been forced to endure ugly partisan idiocy for over a year, and the last few months of it are almost intolerable; normal election years are bad enough, but presidential election years are a kind of evil circus which turns even normal people who pay too much attention to it into raving lunatics. And the worst part of it? Despite the mindless glorification of their own candidate and equally-mindless vilification of the other, most modern US presidential elections have about as much impact on the future of the country as choosing a new color of paint for one's house. Until Americans succeeded in electing a *bona fide* madman to the post, every president going back to Reagan, no matter what his campaign rhetoric, mostly continued the policies of his predecessor once he got in the White House. My wasband says he imagines that on the evening of inauguration day, the new president goes into the Oval Office alone and meets with a mysterious old man in a gray suit who puts a binder on his desk and explains for the next six hours or so exactly how things are going to be.

      While I don't necessarily believe that's *literally* true, it is correct in principle because this country is not run by elected officials, but by an entrenched bureaucracy; even the mad emperor Trump has only expanded the power of that bureaucracy. The "progressive" philosophy of the late

136

Honored in the Breach

19th century held that ordinary people could not be trusted to
run our own lives; instead, we should be governed by
"experts" who would determine what was best for us. As this
mentality took hold over the next few decades, burgeoning
federal and state bureaucracies insinuated or forced their way
into areas of life which had throughout human history been
considered private and personal. Since the people could not
be trusted to choose those who would run these rapidly-
multiplying bureaus (and by the 1930s there were far too
many of them to elect anyhow), they were hired and
progressed upward by supposed "merit", much like the
military. And like the military, they stayed in place when the
elected officials changed. As the federal government
metastasized after World War II, the number, reach and
power of these positions dramatically increased; then, as anti-
discrimination and other employee protection laws
multiplied, the career bureaucrats in those positions became
virtually impossible to fire. The final tipping point came
sometime during the Reagan administration, not because of
anything he did but simply as the end result of the
interactions of layer upon layer of contradictory, vague, ill-
considered legislation, regulation, guidelines and official
procedures. Sometime in the 1980s, the unelected
bureaucracy assumed the real power in Washington, not
through a conscious act (*see page 83*) but merely because
neither ruling party is willing (nor probably even able) to
take the drastic steps necessary to shut it down, chop it into
pieces and destroy every last cell of it with fire so as to
prevent its regeneration. It will continue to grow until it
collapses of its own weight or consumes all available

resources, at which point it will perish and take the current system of government with it.

This is the main reason I don't vote. In a republic, the electorate chooses representatives to act on its behalf; by participating in the system, each voter agrees to abide by the results of the process and tacitly acknowledges that the leaders so elected (and by extension the underlings they appoint and the bureaucrats those underlings hire, including police) have legitimate authority over them. People love to say, "if you don't vote, you have no right to complain," but this is completely backwards: it is the *voters* who have no right to complain, because by signing on to this devil's bargain they agree to be bound by it. In "Your Vote Doesn't Count" (*Reason* magazine, November 2012), Katherine Mangu-Ward explained it this way:

> ...In his 1851 book *Social Statics*, the English radical Herbert Spencer neatly describes the rhetorical jujitsu surrounding voting, consent, and complaint, then demolishes the argument. Say a man votes and his candidate wins. The voter is then "understood to have assented" to the acts of his representative. But what if he voted for the other guy? Well, then, the argument goes, "by taking part in such an election, he tacitly agreed to abide by the decision of the majority." And what if he abstained? "Why then he cannot justly complain...seeing that he made no protest...Curiously enough, it seems that he gave his consent in whatever way he acted—whether he said yes, whether he said no, or whether he remained neuter! A rather awkward doctrine this." Indeed.

The chance of any candidate whose views come within 46 parsecs of mine being nominated to the presidency by either faction of the duopoly is so close to zero as to be mathematically indistinguishable from it, and the chance of a third-party candidate being elected in our current system isn't much higher. Furthermore, even if such a candidate were to be elected to the presidency, the Republicrats wouldn't allow him to accomplish anything. My vote is therefore not merely worthless, but assigned a negative value; it is worth more to me uncast, as a protest against the current system and as a symbolic rejection of the "authorities" produced by that system. For me, voting has become a custom more honored in the breach than the observance.

Like a Horse and Carriage

Love and marriage, love and marriage,
Go together like a horse and carriage. – Sammy Cahn

About 2½ years before *Obergefell v Hodges* was decided, I finally figured out what it is about same-sex marriage rhetoric that irritates me. Now, as a bisexual anarchist I have absolutely nothing against the *concept*, except insofar as I think the government should get out of the marriage business entirely and that all "marriages" should be contracts between two or more consenting adults of any combination of sexes, with the terms, privileges, duration, responsibilities, etc spelled out in writing, and disputes arbitrated under standard contract law. Yet every time I read the arguments of same-sex marriage advocates, especially in the last few years leading up to the decision, I found myself getting annoyed for no reason I could adequately pin down. But one cold morning the week after the 2012 elections I was walking to my barn and it suddenly came to me (and you'd be amazed just how many things come to me during such walks): the culprit is "love" rhetoric, as in calling same-sex marriage "freedom to love" or Google's calling its campaign for the issue "Legalize Love".

For quite some time now the Western world has sunk more and more deeply into the delusion that marriage is "about" love, that love can keep a marriage together by itself, etc. As I wrote in my 2011 essay "Housewife Harlotry",

> ...love is the icing, not the cake...Marriage is first and foremost a socioeconomic relationship, and the modern insistence that love is the be-all and end-all of marriage is one of the primary reasons for...divorce...because couples who share no bond other than the biochemical one we call "romantic love" have no reason to stay together when time and adversity weakens or destroys it. True love is a much more complex emotional bond, but it takes time to develop and rarely does so between people who are not already bound together by other, more mundane bonds such as blood or mutual dependence.

This adolescent refrain of "love love love" (like a scratched Beatles record) whenever the subject of marriage (same-sex or otherwise) comes up gets on my nerves, because for those laboring under that misapprehension all same-sex marriage will do is to slightly increase the divorce rate.

But there's another, more important concern, which is: why is the reason two people choose to live together, sign a contract together or have sex with each other any business of the government's? I find the notion that a contract of mutual economic interdependence can only be drawn up between two people who boink each another to be just as

140

Like a Horse and Carriage

inane, irrational and offensive as same-sex marriage proponents consider the notion that the two parties must be of opposite sexes. For example, why can't two heterosexuals of the same sex make a contract to pool their resources, share insurance, secure inheritance, etc, without having to pretend they sleep together? In the past, marriages were delineated to protect children, not to confer a special state sanction on people sticking their body parts into one another's orifices; since many couples (hetero- or homosexual) nowadays choose to remain childless, why does it matter whether they have sex? And please, don't yammer about "love"; not only is it totally legal to marry for money or other practical concerns, I also think it's a bit hypocritical for a government which spends billions trying to keep some people from getting high to subsidize others making life-altering decisions while under the influence of mind-altering chemicals, merely because those chemicals happen to originate inside their own bodies. Furthermore, it's highly discriminatory to subsidize only sexual love, but not fraternal love.

Governments have no right to set any limits on relations between consenting adults. They should not be able to bar people from having sex, nor to require that parties to certain contracts *must* have sex. They do not have the right to control the gender, number, acts, frequency, duration, terms, reasons, compensation, or any other factors between adults who *do* choose to have sex, nor to harass them for their choices. And they certainly don't have the right to declare that sexual relationships are only for people who are "in love", or to give special preferences to those who are. Though Western tradition of the last couple of centuries increasingly frowns upon marriages contracted for reasons other than romantic love, it is not the state's place to enact such mores into law any more than it would have been its place a century ago to legally require all wheeled vehicles to be drawn by horses. Sammy Cahn was right; love and marriage do go together *exactly* like a horse and carriage: traditionally associated, but not the only conceivable arrangement, and perhaps not even the best one.

Somebody's Daughter

Every girl who worked for me was someone's daughter. It would be…hypocritical…to say, "It's good enough for their daughters, but not for mine". – Becky Adams

In July of 2012, retired UK brothel owner Becky Adams ignited controversy among busybodies, moralists and hypocrites with the simple statement that, like many other people, she wouldn't mind if her daughter followed in her footsteps:

> "Society may judge her but I wouldn't. At least prostitution is an honest profession. I'd much rather she work as an escort than a banker. I couldn't understand her wanting to do something morally wrong, something that could jeopardise someone else…I think my work showed Emilia that the reality of prostitution is just very ordinary. The girls have their shifts and they go to work. They can have a bad day or a quiet day, just like anybody else…prostitution is a service…Emilia has seen…how it can save marriages — how a man whose wife is fighting cancer will visit a prostitute rather than start an affair. She's not shocked by anything as a result…"

Somebody's Daughter

Those who can't understand Adams' position appear to be suffering from what we might call the Fallacy of Universal Mores, the false belief that everyone feels the same way about sex as they do. These people, of whom the "no woman could willingly choose prostitution" crowd is a subset, apparently imagine that those who choose sex work are ashamed of ourselves and hate our lives, and would therefore never want our children to make the same choices we did. They just can't get it through their thick skulls that some women really don't find sex work horrible and degrading, and therefore would not oppose daughters taking up the trade if that was what they wanted to do. Up until quite recently, it wasn't at all unusual for the daughters of sex workers to follow their mothers into the profession; the Ouled-Nail of Algeria (*see "The Ouled Nail" in Volume II*) did it for scores of generations (exactly how long, nobody knows; see "Dance of the Seasons" in *Ladies of the Night* for a fictionalized portrayal). And even among well-adjusted sex workers who say they *would* mind their daughters taking up the work, the usual reason is not anything prohibitionists imagine, but rather the stigma and the dangers resulting from criminalization. Some others (myself included) object not on principle, but because of the belief that a specific daughter is not suited to the work.

But there's another aspect to the "shocked" reactions which is even more indicative of disordered thinking. People who ask, "Would you want your daughter to do it?" aren't concerned with the actual dangers of sex work, because if they were we'd hear it used as an argument against women joining the military, doing police work or participating in dangerous sports like boxing (*see page 131*). Let's set aside for a moment the obvious point that there are lots of things people wouldn't want their daughters doing (smoking, excessive drinking, getting pregnant out of wedlock, working at Wal-Mart, going into politics) which aren't illegal, and the equally obvious fact that we don't get to choose our offspring's occupations (though some certainly try). Let's consider only that people do lots of things their parents wouldn't like, and that most whores have parents who would be upset and appalled at the choice. It's not your decision whether your daughter becomes a hooker; it's hers. And if she does make that choice (which 1% of all Western daughters do for some portion of their lives), do you really want her hounded by cops, forced into dangerous situations, unable to seek legal recourse if she's robbed or raped, and branded as a pariah for life because of it? Or would you rather she have the ability to repent what you see as her mistake and leave the job later if she chose? Finally, is it worth rejecting your own flesh and blood for making a decision with which you disagree, and which hurt nobody except (in your opinion) her? My mother thought so, which is why she hasn't spoken to me since the autumn of 1997, and therefore doesn't know about all the people I've helped and the respect I've earned in my field.

Presumably, those who cannot comprehend why a whore would accept her daughter's decision to practice the same profession believe that the mother should adamantly denounce her own decisions (thus demonstrating that she has poor judgment and is therefore incompetent to give advice on the subject). Or perhaps they think she should be a hypocrite, indulging in the common parental "Do as I say, not as I do." In either case, they apparently hold that a mother should reject her daughter for making a decision she disagrees with, a course of action which (as I can affirm) never results in a desirable outcome. I suppose I shouldn't be surprised at the lack of thought demonstrated by their reactions, though; after all, these are the same people who support paternalistic laws whose consequences are far more damaging than those of the behaviors they supposedly "protect" people from.

A False Dichotomy

To depend upon a profession is a less odious form of slavery than to depend upon a father. – Virginia Woolf

Those prohibitionists who favor "feminist" anti-sex rhetoric claim that all sex workers are helpless victims of male dominance, slaves to "patriarchal oppressors", and even many rational but ill-informed people have come to believe enough of the propaganda that they think "most" of us are coerced; even some sex workers have bought into this notion sufficiently that they believe there are two and only two kinds of whores, free-willed high-dollar independent escorts and pimped, coerced slaves. This, of course, is pure poppycock; human relationships, and even free will itself, are never as cut-and-dried as the anti-sex feminists or other Manichean dualists want to pretend. The notion that all whores (or all workers, or all humans) must be either free or enslaved is a false duality which ignores both the realities of the human condition and the necessities of material existence.

The only people who can truly claim to have made an absolutely free choice to do any kind of work are the Paris Hiltons of the world, those who have a guaranteed inheritance, income and secured future no matter what they choose to do with the present. Every other person has no choice but to work in some fashion; the choice not to work at all simply doesn't exist unless one considers starvation an option. The choice, then, boils down to what *kind* of work one is able and willing to do. I'd love to be paid to do what I'm doing right now – namely, writing about whatever I want to write whenever I want to write it, without answering to anybody – but in the real world very few people who aren't already bestselling authors get that opportunity. Conversely, there are lots of things I'm quite able to do, but wouldn't be willing to do regularly for pay. I eventually settled on sex work as the best way to get everything I wanted career-wise (high income, flexibility, freedom from arbitrary schedules and rules, no bosses, and no confiscatory "withholding") while doing something I was already good at. In other words, escorting provided the greatest advantages for the least compromise. Eventually I made a slightly different choice, namely housewifery, but in my mind that's just another form of sex work. And when that gig ended (amicably) and I needed to go back to earning my own income, there was no question that I'd go back to harlotry.

And I'm not remotely alone; millions of women all over the world and throughout history have chosen prostitution for similar reasons to mine. Each of them took stock of her assets, needs and preferences and decided that whoring was the best way to accomplish her goals. The anti-sex feminists claim that only women with no other choice decide to become sex workers, but that's as ridiculous an assertion as it is simplistic; there are many, many poor, unskilled women in this world who would never choose whoredom, and many, many educated, talented women who do. Harlotry is not right for everyone (*see page 52*), but then neither is teaching, nursing, motherhood, secretarial work or any other career. All but a very small number of us *must* work, and everyone who isn't actually compelled by force to do some particular form of work has *some* choice, however limited it may be.

But what about those who are literally compelled? Obviously there are cases like the "comfort women", but in modern times such forcible enslavement is comparatively rare. Some of what the rescue industry calls "slavery" is actually debt bondage (a condition with which I daresay much of the American middle class is intimately familiar), but some of it isn't even that; as the anthropologist Dr. Laura Agustín has discussed on numerous occasions, a great deal of the "trafficking" mythology is rooted in the racist assumption that people (especially women) from developing countries are childlike simpletons who can easily be manipulated by oh-so-superior Westerners, and so they are "enslaved" by the evil white men and can only be "rescued" by the good white men. The "rescuers" presume that any foreign woman selling sex in Europe or the US is "trafficked", when in reality the majority of them made a choice, and the people who are labeled as "traffickers" are usually simply those who transported them and/or arranged for false papers. Not to be outdone, the fanatics are now trying to claim that the reason migrants deny being enslaved is not because it's the truth, but because they're suffering from "Stockholm Syndrome"! They simply cannot accept that some people really do prefer doing sex work to being virtual slaves in a sweatshop, and that they migrate not because they're passively "trafficked" but because they're actively looking for a better life than they could find in their own countries.

Of course, pointing any of this out to a "sex trafficking" fanatic will merely trigger an avalanche of "enslaved children" rhetoric. But even that isn't as it's represented; as I've pointed out before, very few underage sex workers in the entire US report having been coerced into the trade, and their average age at the time they begin is 16 rather than the 13 claimed by fetishists (*see page 45*). Considering that 16 is of legal age to consent to sex in 39 American states and many nations, I hardly think that qualifies as a "child". And in the developing world, 16 is in many cases an adult no matter what the UN may declare; even in the West the concept of 18 as a "magic number" of adulthood is a relatively recent one, and in most of the world such a distinction simply doesn't exist. Despite the efforts of ivory-tower idealists to declare adolescents "innocent children", the fact is that legal minors often do leave home, sometimes with good reason (such as physical or sexual abuse, or parental mistreatment because they're LGBT), and many of them survive by selling sex…with nary a pimp nor "trafficker" in sight.

And what *of* the pimps? Even though they're pretty rare, certainly we can all agree that for a man to force a woman into prostitution and then take her money is wrong, can't we? Well, in the cases where it really *is* like that I'd agree, but the percentage of whores with abusive, controlling pimps is very similar to the percentage of women with abusive, controlling husbands or boyfriends (*see page 76*); some men are just bastards and some women are (for whatever reason) willing to put up with it, and whores are no exception. At the most basic level, what is a pimp but a man who is supported by a woman's work? Sex work is work, so a prostitute supporting a pimp who lacks a literal hold on her is no morally different from any other woman supporting her

A False Dichotomy

husband or boyfriend with any other kind of work. And though I wouldn't work to support an able-bodied man, I also wouldn't want it to be illegal; people have the right to make their own decisions, even if I or others think those decisions are bad, stupid or self-destructive. Furthermore, most of the people accused of "pimping", "pandering", "sex trafficking", "living on the avails", etc are nothing like the stereotyped pimp of prohibitionist propaganda, and many aren't even male; the charge is most often inflicted on partners, drivers, roommates, landlords, bookers and even friends. When whores work together for safety, convenience or special requests (some gents enjoy seeing two ladies at once), they may be charged with pimping each other, and it's not unusual for dependent adult family members (such as university-age children or invalid parents) to be charged under "avails" laws as well. In some jurisdictions we've even seen the blatant absurdity of sex workers being charged with "trafficking" themselves to increase the "crime" from misdemeanor to felony, making them simultaneously "victim" and "pimp".

Real life is not like a silent melodrama; the baddies do not all wear black hats and sport waxed moustaches, and many of the women who are tied to the railroad tracks are there because they consented to be and will not appreciate ham-fisted attempts at "rescue". There is a whole spectrum between the party girl whoring herself for thrills and the chained sex slave, and the number of women at the one end is no higher than that at the other. The vast majority of us, like the vast majority of the human race, exist in the murky grey area between absolute freedom and abject slavery, trying our best to balance the pursuit of happiness with the toil necessary for survival.

Harlots of the Bible

Verily I say unto you, that the publicans and the harlots go into the kingdom of God before you. – Matthew 21:31

Many people would expect a discussion of this topic to begin with St. Mary Magdalene; the Bible, however, provides no evidence for the legend of Mary as a harlot, repentant or otherwise. The legend seems to derive from a sermon in 591 wherein Pope Gregory the Great identified her as such, possibly by identification with the "adulterous woman" whom Jesus rescues from being stoned in the 8th chapter of John. But even if the most famous Biblical whore probably wasn't one, there are a number of other ladies of my profession to be found in its pages.

The first notable mention occurs in Genesis 38, and as might be expected of an episode taking place about the 15th century BCE the harlot concerned was a temple prostitute...or to be exact, a woman *disguised* as a temple prostitute. The Hebrew Levirate law required that a man marry his brother's childless widow so the dead brother might have descendants to inherit his name and property, and the widow would have children to support her in old age. The patriarch Judah had three sons: Er, Onan and Shelah, but Er died suddenly before giving his wife, Tamar, any children. Er's younger brother, Onan, married her as duty demanded, but he hated his dead brother and refused to give him descendants; though he had sex with Tamar he withdrew before ejaculation and *"spilled it on the ground, lest that he should give seed to his brother"* – (Genesis 38:9). Yahweh was very unhappy about this combination rape and dereliction of duty and accordingly slew Onan; weirdly

150

enough, Christian preachers of the early 18th century used this as evidence that God disliked masturbation ("spilling seed on the ground") and referred to the act as "onanism", thus demonstrating that they entirely misunderstood the nature of Onan's transgression.

In any case, Shelah should have next inherited the duty but he was too young to marry, so Judah asked Tamar to wait; however, when the boy came of age the father did not uphold his promise. The clever girl therefore travelled to a nearby town whither Judah had driven his sheep to have them shorn, and disguised herself as a veiled Canaanite temple prostitute (the Hebrew word used is *kedeshah*, a sacred prostitute, rather than *zonah*, a common one) in order to entice her father-in-law to hire her. The plan worked; he promised to pay her a kid from his flock, and as a bond he left his signet ring, bracelets and staff. Of course, she had no interest in payment; what she wanted was the child due her, so after the act was done she left without waiting for the kid to be delivered, and when her pregnancy began to show three months later she presented the identifying items as proof of her child's lawful parentage. Judah confessed that he had been tricked into doing his duty, Tamar had twins and everything worked out for the best: the sons became the ancestors of the tribe of Judah, i.e. the Jews.

Tamar was not the only Biblical harlot with important descendants. In the second chapter of Joshua two Hebrew spies lodged in the house of a harlot named Rahab while in Jericho, and she hid them from searchers in return for their promise that when they invaded her city she and her family would be spared. Why did she do this for two strangers? Self-interest was certainly a major factor, but hospitality laws probably came into play as well; in the ancient Middle East a host had a sacred responsibility to those under his roof, which is why Lot was willing to turn his own daughters over to the Sodomite rape-gang in Genesis 19:4-8 rather than give up the disguised angels who were his guests. Also, Rahab seems to have been rather disgusted by the spineless response of her countrymen to news of the Hebrew victories; she tells the spies, *"your terror is fallen upon us, and that all the inhabitants of the land faint because of you...neither did there remain any more courage in any man, because of you"* (Joshua 2:9-11). In any case, Joshua kept the pact to which his spies had committed him and Rahab and her family were spared; she married one of the Hebrews and became the ancestress of either several prophets or of Jesus himself, depending on which Biblical scholar one chooses to believe.

The First Book of Kings (chapter 3, verses 16-28), tells the famous story of King Solomon's judgment over two harlots who shared a house; one overlaid her baby and he died, so she switched the body for the other woman's child. The King ordered that the living baby be split with a sword and half given to each, whereupon the real mother instantly renounced the infant to save its life. But there's a strange detail at the end of the story; we are told *"all Israel heard of the judgment which the king had judged; and they feared the king"*, which is a strange reaction unless one recognizes the politics behind it. Solomon, you see, was not the rightful heir; he was the son of David's concubine Bathsheba. The throne should have gone to his elder brother Adonijah, but Solomon was the cleverer politician and contrived a coup. Immediately upon taking the throne he spread the story of the judgment over the harlots, which was in actuality a parable: the wrongful mother (Solomon) was willing to let the baby (Israel) be split with a sword (divided by civil war), but the

152

rightful mother (Adonijah) could avoid the butchery by relinquishing parental (royal) rights. No wonder the people were afraid!

In Solomon's parable Israel was the child of a whore, but by Ezekiel's time (early 6th century BCE) she was portrayed as a whore herself. Ezekiel repeatedly prophesied the destruction of Jerusalem for its "betrayal" of Mosaic Law, and one of his parables painted the now-divided Hebrew kingdom (northern Samaria and southern Judah) as a pair of harlot sisters who enjoy their work *entirely* too much. He describes their "whoredoms" in great and lurid detail, mentioning several times that their clients bruised their tits (Ezekiel 23:3, 8 and 21), and he seems especially fascinated with the size of their clients' penises and the volume of their seminal discharge (*"For she doted upon their paramours, whose flesh is as the flesh of asses, and whose issue is like the issue of horses."* – Ezekiel 23:20). I'll bet you never studied *that* passage in catechism or Sunday school!

But what about the woman whose name is practically synonymous with "whore", namely Jezebel? She was not a sex worker, but rather a Phoenician princess who married King Ahab of Israel and dutifully built temples to her own gods in her adopted land, thus earning the wrath of the fanatical prophet Elisha. After Ahab's death Elisha backed a usurper who overthrew the rightful heir and ordered Queen Jezebel's servants to hurl her from a palace window to her death (2 Kings 9). The association of her name with harlotry appears to derive from the fact that when she knew death was near, she made up her face and dressed in full royal regalia so as to die a queen; plus the fact that Elisha, like Ezekiel in later centuries, used the word "whoredom" as a metaphor for

153

turning from Yahweh to other gods. Of course, Jezebel wasn't a Hebrew so her adherence to her native gods can hardly be considered apostasy, but little details like that (and the fact that in Phoenicia, makeup wasn't considered the exclusive province of harlots as it was in Israel) don't matter much to homicidal religious maniacs.

Nor to mystical visionaries like St. John the Divine, who in the 1st century CE portrayed Jezebel as a sort of succubus: "*...thou sufferest that woman Jezebel, which calleth herself a prophetess, to teach and to seduce my servants to commit fornication, and to eat things sacrificed unto idols. And I gave her space to repent of her fornication; and she repented not. Behold, I will cast her into a bed, and them that commit adultery with her into great tribulation, except they repent of their deeds.*" (Revelation 2:20-22) John was one of those Christians who followed in the footsteps of the Hebrew prophets by using whores as symbols for everything filthy; the most famous is of course the Whore of Babylon from Revelation 17:

And there came one of the seven angels...saying unto me, Come hither; I will shew unto thee the judgment of the great whore that sitteth upon many waters: With whom the kings of the earth have committed fornication, and the inhabitants of the earth have been made drunk with the wine of her fornication...and I saw a woman sit upon a scarlet coloured beast, full of names of blasphemy, having seven heads and ten horns. And the woman was arrayed in purple and scarlet color, and decked with gold and precious stones and pearls, having a golden cup in her hand full of abominations and filthiness of her fornication: And upon her forehead [was] a name written, *Mystery, Babylon the Great, The Mother of Harlots and Abominations of the Earth.*"

Though modern Christian fundamentalists believe the Whore of Babylon to be a literal person, this is a fairly recent interpretation; most Biblical scholars believe she was a symbol for Rome, and Martin Luther and other leaders of the Reformation taught that she was a symbol for the Catholic Church. But whichever interpretation one accepts, with Babylon the transformation is complete: the whores of the oldest parts of the Bible are strong, realistic and positively-portrayed women, but as the centuries wore on and women's status sank the harlot became a symbol for increasingly negative and abstract concepts.

Imagination Pinned Down

Memory is imagination pinned down. – Mason Cooley

Many people believe that human memory is like a video camera, in that it objectively records perceived events and stores the images and sounds in some sort of indelible medium which can be erased, mislaid or purposefully hidden, but never distorted; the whole principle of "eyewitness testimony" in our legal system derives from this belief. But as a great deal of research going back to the beginning of modern psychology has demonstrated, it simply isn't true. The human mind doesn't passively record events as a camera does; memory is an active and dynamic process which retains information by fitting it into schemata, mental frameworks which shape our thinking and give meaning to perceptions. For example, a chess master shown a board in the middle of a real game can quickly memorize the positions of the pieces with a high degree of accuracy and retention, but if shown a board in which the pieces are randomly arranged he cannot memorize the positions any better than anyone else. This is because in the former case the board layout fits neatly into his highly-developed schema of chess rules and strategy, while in the latter case it's just a bunch of objects with no discernible order or meaning.

As Victor Frankl observed, human beings have a deep need for meaning; we look for order in even the most chaotic arrangement of objects or events. The same psychological mechanism which causes us to find pictures in Rorschach's inkblots also causes us to fit memories into the complex web of schemata by which we interpret the world. And just as we ignore those topological elements of a cloud or inkblot which do not fit the meaning our minds have imposed upon it, so do we forget or distort elements of a memory which fail to conform to the schema in which we have embedded it, or even *invent elements which were not in reality present*, but which the schema predicts should be. This is an extremely important point, so I'll repeat it: The human mind often completely fabricates memories in order to impose conformity with one's *weltanschauung*. One simple example involves police lineups: people will often identify the man whom police imply (subtly or overtly) is their preferred suspect because they believe police to be expert assessors of guilt who would never implicate someone falsely, and this schema of police authority and infallibility actually shapes their memories, sometimes to the point of identifying a person who is later proven to look absolutely *nothing* like the actual criminal.

Traumatic events tend to induce psychological imbalance which renders the victim even more subject to

156

Imagination Pinned Down

suggestion by perceived authority figures, which is how False Memory Syndrome develops; a person suffering from depression, anxiety or even nightmares seeks therapy (or has it forced upon her by a court or family) and develops a psychological dependence on a manipulative (and usually agenda-driven) "therapist" who convinces her that all of her problems result from childhood sexual abuse, and then proceeds to "help" her "recover" those memories as one might dig through a closet for a lost videotape. But memory does not work that way; in reality this procedure does not "recover" existing memories but creates completely new ones which conform to the therapist's narrative, and reconfigures existing ones to agree with the confabulations. The syndrome was largely responsible for the Satanic Panic, and also for witchcraft hysteria of past centuries; in the latter case the pressure to reshape memories was inflicted by religious authorities and by the culture as a whole rather than by individual agents such as therapists.

It is important to recognize that people who form false memories are neither stupid nor weak-willed, and their memories are not lies but essentially misfiled fantasies. Everyone files memories for recall by linking them to other cognitive artifacts (memories, ideas, thoughts, beliefs, etc), and when a dream, delusion, fantasy or the like is filed in the same way as a memory the brain treats it as one; moreover, when the false memory is linked to positive reinforcement (such as the approval of a group or authority figure), it is apt to become even more persistent than the memories of real events which lack such powerful associations. If the false memories serve as the passport into an identity group, they are likely to become the person's most intense memories because they form an essential keystone of self-identification.

There are a number of psychological criteria shared by the majority of those who are unusually susceptible to remembering experiences that did not happen in objective reality (including alien abductions, demonic possession, cultic victimization, etc); research conducted on such people has revealed that they tend to share a majority of the following characteristics:

* *They are easy to hypnotize*
* *As children they played in a fantasy world*
* *They believed in fairies, guardian angels, etc.*
* *As children they had invisible playmates*
* *They spend a significant part of their time fantasizing*
* *They often believe they have psychic abilities*
* *Most have had out-of-body experiences*
* *They often believe they have healing powers*
* *They are subject to hypnagogic experiences*
* *They have very vivid dreams*
* *They have good memories*
* *They receive messages from unknown forces*

Though everyone is susceptible to memory distortion to some degree, those who are so vulnerable that they can be readily convinced that bizarre, unusual, fantastic or even impossible things really did happen to them are called "Fantasy Prone Persons"; they make up roughly 4% of the population. Most FPPs are also extremely sexual; many of them can achieve orgasm through fantasy alone, and their false memories usually have a strong sexual element, often with powerful BDSM overtones. Have you ever wondered why supposed "memories" of witchcraft, Satanic ritual abuse,

Imagination Pinned Down

alien abduction and the like often include sexual elements, especially ones in which the person was raped, subjected to bondage, sexually tortured, mind controlled or "hypnotized", etc? It's because they all come from the same shadowy part of the brain, and the identity of the abusers (and other particulars of the false memory) are just window dressing. Studies demonstrate that these details depend on the individuals' beliefs and associates: traditionally-religious FPPs are likely to believe they've been possessed by demons or sexually abused by cultists; those with a strong interest in science fiction or UFOs are likely to identify their imaginary tormentors as aliens; and women with an unhappy history of sex work, or who become too immersed in "sex trafficking" porn, remember lurid experiences of vast pimp networks and dozens of clients a day, etc.

Next time you see one of these "survivor" narratives, compare it to the now-discredited accounts of Satanic ritual abuse and the widely-ridiculed tales of alien medical experiments. Many "survivors" report savage beatings, being shut for days in scorpion-filled sewage barrels (*see "Follow Your Bliss" on my blog*) or being dragged down the street behind a pimp's or client's car, yet never have any permanent injuries to show for it…just as the McMartin Preschool children bore no scars from anal knife rapes, and alien medical examinations likewise leave no marks. Consider the eerie similarity of "survivor" narratives and their convergence since the dawn of "sex trafficking" hysteria, just as Satanic abuse narratives resemble those from 16th-century witch trials and alien abduction tales converged after the release of *Close Encounters of the Third Kind*.

The Essential Maggie McNeill

Think also about the impossible logistics of the situations described by people like Theresa Flores, who claims to have been "abducted" from her upper-middle-class family home every night for two years and forced to prostitute herself, yet was freed every morning to attend school; supposedly neither her parents nor siblings ever heard her come or go, nor did she ever show any signs of sleep deprivation or psychological trauma sufficient to raise any suspicion. The same miraculous immunity to detection and circumstance protected the McMartin cultists: no parent, delivery person or other outsider ever showed up while everyone was downstairs in the secret Satanic temple, and no child ever suffered trauma or said a word about seeing people fly until the "investigators" questioned them. And nobody else in the neighborhoods from which alien abductees are taken ever see or hear ships, aliens, or hypnotized levitating test subjects. It's clear that people who recount such stories believe them, and can therefore easily pass the polygraph tests which are sometimes used to prop up their unbelievable tales. They are not lying in the strict sense, because they really do remember these events; however, as the dreamlike (or nightmarish) character of their memories and the lack of physical evidence amply demonstrate, their adventures took place in an unreal Twilight Zone rather than in the mundane world where normal events occur.

Readers interested in a deeper exploration of this topic are invited to download "Mind-Witness Testimony" from the Resources page of my blog; it's a research paper I published in the Albany Government Law Review *in 2014, with copious footnotes. Readers are further invited to look up terms from this essay, and to peruse the work of memory expert Elizabeth Loftus.*

The Kisaeng

Oh that I might capture the essence of this deep midwinter night
And fold it softly into the waft of a spring-moon quilt,
Then fondly uncoil it the night my beloved returns. –
Hwang Jini

    Sex work is so stigmatized, slandered and hidden in modern Western society that it is difficult for most modern Westerners to comprehend just how normal it was in pre-industrial societies, and how woven into the fabric of those societies. Nowadays we are wont to draw sharp lines between prostitutes, mistresses, girlfriends, actresses, dancers, masseuses and other groups of women, but for most of human history the distinctions between various types of non-wives from whom men could obtain sex were blurry at best. Consider that courtesans such as the Madame de Pompadour and Jane Shore were still considered harlots despite the fact that all their liaisons were long-term and their total lifetime count of sex partners was lower than most modern women (who would be extremely offended to be called whores) rack up before graduating from university; also remember that working-class women from Roman times until well into the 20th century often supplemented their meager earnings by selling sex on the side, and you'll begin to understand why the idea of the prostitute as a specific, "fallen" kind of woman only dates to the 19th century (and seems so ridiculous to those who know anything about it). That's why modern assertions that certain historical types of women (such as *geisha*) were "not prostitutes" are so absurd and wrongheaded; even if these women did not openly
161

advertise and sell sex to a large number of clients, there is no doubt that compensated sex was on the menu for at least some clients, and that in Christian Europe they absolutely would have been classified as whores.

The *kisaeng* of feudal Korea are a case in point. Though some authorities insist that they were definitely not prostitutes, or that only the lowest of the three classes of *kisaeng* were, or that only *some* did that job, the distinction simply isn't a useful one. Whether a given woman took money for sex or not was wholly immaterial to her status; that was always *cheonmin*, the lowest caste of Korean society except for the *baekjeong* (untouchables). The *cheonmin* included members of all "unclean" professions including butchers, entertainers, jailers, metalworkers, prostitutes, shamans, shoemakers and sorcerers; they were not all slaves, but slaves were drawn from this caste. *Kisaeng* were technically slaves, and after 1650 they were all owned by the government; due to their high degree of training they were treated much better than ordinary slaves, but they were still owned by the state, and the price of freedom was so high it could only be paid by wealthy men (if such a man wanted one as a concubine).

There were three ways a girl could become a *kisaeng*: she could be born to a *kisaeng* mother (since caste was hereditary), sold to a *kisaeng* house by parents who could not afford to raise her, or drop out of the upper classes due to some unforgiveable breach of the complex and rigid Korean social rules. Training started young (as early as eight) and their careers were extremely short: they usually began active duty about 15, peaked about 17, and retired by age 22. During the Joseon Dynasty (1392-1897) this was codified into law; they were forced to retire from entertainment duties (including prostitution, singing and such) by 30, though they

The Kisaeng

could continue working at non-entertainment tasks until 50. Like the *geisha* of Japan, *kisaeng* were trained in poetry, music, dance, art, conversation and the like; in fact, one particular poetic form (the *sijo*) came to be associated with them, and some famous examples are basically advertisements intended to entice gentlemen to buy their sexual services. But some *kisaeng* were also trained in needlework and medicine; since Korean doctors were not permitted to see noblewomen naked, their examination and hands-on treatment was the province of medical *kisaeng* under the direction of a doctor. The *haengsu*, highest of the three tiers of kisaeng, were in charge of training after they retired; those of the two lower tiers who were not taken as concubines generally retired by working as seamstresses, food preparers, tavern keepers or the like. Though some *kisaeng* became wealthy enough to support themselves, this did not happen nearly as frequently as among European courtesans.

Korean society was strict and regimented at every level, and the *kisaeng* were no exception; they were registered and forced to report twice a month to a bureaucrat called the *hojang* to ensure that they could not flee servitude without soon being missed. Their day-to-day affairs, however, (including disputes with clients) were supervised by the *haengsu*. Prior to the ascent of the Joseon Dynasty this was much looser, but the Joseons were Confucian and thus deeply enamored of hierarchy and regimentation. For the first two centuries of Joseon rule there were frequent calls for the abolition of the *kisaeng*, but wiser heads always prevailed because it was understood that without sex workers, officials would be much more likely to satisfy their extramarital urges with other men's wives. The subjugation of all *kisaeng* to strict government control was thus a compromise with those who imagined society could do without whores, just as modern legalization schemes are. After 1650 some *kisaeng* were assigned to a specific government office; these were called *gwan-gi*, and though officeholders were strictly forbidden from having sex with them, in practice they were usually expected and often forced to provide sex to these bureaucrats (because some things never change). Many *kisaeng* who were not bound directly to government service had a *gibu*, or boyfriend; he got sex and companionship in exchange for protection, presents and economic support. Most *gibu* were lesser officials, military officers or the like, and though they had no legal status they sometimes became very possessive and pimpish; there were even cases in which they got into fights with their girlfriends' clients, though obviously this was considered extremely rude and might result in the *kisaeng* breaking off the relationship. Over time *gibu* became more popular, and by the beginning of the 19th century it was rare to find a *kisaeng* without one.

Throughout the late 19th century, Korea was destabilized by interference from China, Japan, France, the UK and the US. The Sino-Japanese War (1894-95) resulted in increased Japanese dominance over Korea, and one of the reforms the Japanese encouraged was the abolition of the entire class system, including slavery. This technically freed the *kisaeng*, but (as so often happens when slaves are freed *en masse* by decree), many of them continued in servitude for the rest of their lives, but without the legal protections of their former status. Some went to work as what Westerners typically think of as prostitutes, and today the term *kisaeng* is sometimes used to mean a whore who specifically caters to foreigners. There are a few of the traditional houses still left,

The Kisaeng

but since most of the songs, dances and such were passed down by oral tradition, they have been lost forever.

Idealized *kisaeng* appear frequently in South Korean historical fiction (much as the *geisha* do in Japan), but North Korea's communist government is so hostile to prostitution that it labels all descendents of *kisaeng* (of whom there are a sizeable number, since Pyongyang was once home to the greatest *kisaeng* school) as having "tainted blood".

Unfortunately, courtesan denial (*see "Profanation" in volume II*) is not rare nowadays; those who insist that sex workers of historical times were somehow fundamentally different from their modern descendants reveal not only a pathological aversion to human sexuality and a deep misunderstanding of human nature, but also an appalling ignorance of the truth about selling sex in any era. Courtesans throughout history would laugh at anyone who claimed that education automatically removed a woman from whoredom; the many who were talented singers, poets and writers would likewise ridicule the notion that artistic training somehow disqualified her from harlotry. They, the *kisaeng*, and modern sex workers all know what so many pathetic moderns deny: a person is not what she does to make money, no matter how much repressive governments want to pretend she is.

Magic Formulae

A man bears beliefs as a tree bears apples.
– Ralph Waldo Emerson

Every profession has its superstitions, and those falling under the general heading of entertainment – acting, sports, music, sex work and others – are among the worst. Athletes have various taboos about their equipment and some won't change their clothes during a winning streak; actors won't say the phrase "good luck" or mention the play *Macbeth* backstage for fear of drawing down disaster; musicians often have lucky charms or pre-show rituals. Since one of the greatest harms which can befall a whore is to be arrested, there are a plethora of magical rituals, formulae or prohibitions which are used by the superstitious to ward off that possibility. Not one of these has even the slightest basis in reality, but many swear by them and cannot be convinced that they do absolutely nothing to reveal a cop, prevent arrest or serve as a defense in court.

Probably the most common of these superstitions is the "cop test"; many hookers believe that there are certain things a cop is not allowed to do (such as take off his shoes, display his penis, feel her tits, etc), and therefore if a man will do one of those things he isn't a cop. Probably the most absurd of these is also the most common: it is believed (by many drug users as well as whores) that if a cop is asked the question "are you a cop?" or "are you affiliated with law enforcement?" or whatever, he has to answer truthfully. These tests are doubly ridiculous because even if they were true in the first place (which they aren't), a cop could still simply lie in the police report and in court (*see "Under*

166

Magic Formulae

Duress" in volume II) to say he didn't do whatever it was he wasn't supposed to do. This is why that other common ritual, the payment ceremony, is just as useless as the cop test: if you let a cop in your door or walk into his, it doesn't matter whether he hands you the money in an envelope or a roll, whether you count it in front of him or not, whether you pick it up or leave it lying on the nightstand, or even whether he gives it to you at all; the police report will say you agreed specifically to perform certain sex acts for a set sum, no matter what you actually did or said. As the expression goes, "you can beat the rap, but you can't beat the ride"; if you meet a cop and he wants to arrest you he will do so, even if you aren't even a sex worker, and no magical formula will prevent that.

The notion that certain rites, gestures and words will protect those who use them from malevolent beings is an ancient one, as is the complementary idea that these creatures cannot do perfectly ordinary things that humans can do with ease. Vampires cannot pass running water, go out in the daytime or enter a house without permission; they are revealed by mirrors and repelled by crosses and garlic. Devils cannot pass through certain magical inscriptions and must abide by the letter of any pact to which they agree. Fairies are repelled by salt and iron, and can only gain power over mortals who venture away from known paths or break certain rules. Why do people believe these things? Why were the monsters of folklore not basically unlimited and virtually unstoppable like those in so many modern movies, and why do people insist on believing that the power of modern villains is bounded by these same kinds of mystical geases and taboos? It's because we need to sleep at night.

The Essential Maggie McNeill

Vampires, devils and faeries were very real to our ancestors, unlike the fictional villains of modern movies; you know very well that Jason and Chucky and Freddy Krueger and the xenomorph of *Alien* aren't real, so it doesn't matter if there are no limits on their power. But if you believed that they *were* real, and you lived in a thatched cottage that wouldn't keep out a determined dog (much less a werewolf), you had *better* believe there were rules the monsters had to follow and wards to keep them away, or else you'd live in a perpetual state of fear.

Modern harlots are like those peasants of earlier times; we are surrounded by powerful predatory fiends lying in wait to pounce on the unwary victim in order to drag her off to their lair. So it shouldn't be terribly surprising that many of us choose to believe that there is a mirror or incantation that will dissolve their disguises and reveal the corrupt beasts beneath, or a charm that will offer protection to the one who knows how to use it. Unfortunately, we are at a disadvantage in comparison to our ancestors: while their magical wards never failed because the monsters they were intended to foil never truly existed in the first place, the threats to our freedom and safety are very real...and the magical formulae to which we cling are utterly powerless against them.

168

An Older Profession Than
You May Have Thought

Not every woman is a prostitute, but prostitution is the natural apotheosis of the feminine attitude.
– Georges Bataille

One of the fascinatingly stupid statements some prohibitionists make about prostitution is that it's "unnatural". I assume this is some alternate meaning of the word "unnatural" with which I am unfamiliar; apparently in this case it means "something the speaker dislikes." Harlotry, based as it is on the pre-human principle of barter, is a helluva lot more natural than marriage and a lot of other things these silly asses have no issue with, and it has been observed in several other species besides ours.

How can that be, you might ask, when only humans have money? If you think that, it's because you fail to grok what money actually is. It is true that only humans have *currency*, the symbolic representation of money, but all species which rely on some limited resource such as food do indeed have money, though we may not call it that. And when a female gives sex to a male in order to obtain some of his resources via barter, she has performed an act of prostitution. For a good example of this we need look no farther than our closest relatives, the chimpanzees.

Like humans, chimpanzees are naturally omnivorous; they need both animal and vegetable food to be healthy, and though the vegetable matter is easily obtained and therefore cheap, chimps will go to considerable lengths to add animal protein to their diet. One way in which they do this is by "fishing" for ants or termites by inserting long sticks into their nests and licking off the insects which climb onto the stick, but as you can imagine this requires a great deal of effort for very little satisfaction. Larger animals are therefore valuable to the chimp who can catch them, and since chimps particularly relish the meat of small monkeys these are *especially* valuable. Researchers have observed male chimp hunters sharing such a kill with their friends, and when a female chimp sees a male doing this she may approach him to offer sex, receiving in payment a piece of the precious meat. Female primate offers male primate sex in direct exchange for a small portion of his resources; that sure sounds like prostitution to me!

Taking this shared behavior into consideration, it seems likely that the "world's oldest profession" is much older than most people might imagine; five million years older, in fact, since that is the age of our last common ancestor with the chimp. It has even been suggested that the universal human custom of a male offering a female food as part of courtship (whether in the form of a primitive hunter bringing her a kill or a modern man taking her to dinner) may also descend from the ancient food-for-sex transaction; it is merely more thoroughly disguised by ritual than prostitution is. Another exact parallel can be seen in the fact that male chimps who share meat with females even when they *aren't* looking for sex (i.e. wealthy, generous ones) mate more often and with a better selection than those who are poor and/or stingy.

Nor are primates the only creatures ever to evolve the pragmatic money-for-sex transaction; Adelie penguins (*Pygoscelis adeliae*) have their own independent tradition, using their own scarce resource as a medium of exchange. These penguins usually mate for life, and in mating season each couple builds a nest of stones to keep their eggs warm and dry. The entire flock clusters in one area with those of highest social rank in the center, while low-status single males are pushed to the periphery just as they are in many other species (including humans). Ironically, this puts the single males in a good position to find choice stones because the center of the area gets picked over quickly. The bachelors therefore build nests themselves, then sit in them and wait.

What happens next is this: if a couple within the flock cannot find sufficient stones to complete a nest, the husband will remain behind to guard the incomplete nest from stone-thieves while his wife waddles off to find a horny bachelor sitting on a pile of good nesting stones. She then flirts with him in her penguiny fashion, and if he responds she presents herself for mating; after he takes what he wants he allows her to take a choice stone and waddle back to her nest with it. Some bachelors demand sex for each stone, while other clients allow their harlots to return for as many stones as they like without having to put out again. But not all of these penguin prostitutes are honest ones; some are actually practitioners of cash-and-dash! One of these nasty little trollops will tease her victim until he jumps off his nest to have her, then she grabs one of his rocks and runs! If he catches her he will beat her and reclaim his stone, but some of them do manage to get away. As in human society, the honest version of the transaction is advantageous to all parties; the female gets resources she needs, and the male gets sex he otherwise would not have. A penguin whore will often go back to the same clients again and again, and if her husband dies before the next breeding season (which happens quite often in the harsh and dangerous Antarctic environment) she will usually choose one of her regulars as her new husband.

Obviously, it's a mistake to attribute anything remotely resembling human thoughts and motives to invertebrates, but there are a few arthropods whose behavior does sort of resemble prostitution in a superficial way. Insects and spiders don't experience anything like what we would call "pleasure"; their nervous systems are of an extremely primitive order and they are not in any way conscious of any motivation for doing the things they do. But when the complexities are stripped away, male bugs seek sex for the same reason as their two- and four-legged counterparts: In order to impregnate females and thereby pass on their genetic legacy. The only difference is that more complex creatures cannot simply be programmed to act in a certain way; Nature had to find some better means to motivate higher animals than "Because I'm the Mother, that's why!" And so sexual pleasure was born, and until the invention of birth control made non-reproductive sex a reality, males were induced to do Nature's work by seeking to gratify their own desires.

Many arthropods don't even have sex in the sense we understand it; males merely generate a sperm packet which they try to attach to the female's body without her noticing, and given sufficient time the sperm passes through her pores and enters her reproductive system. If the female discovers this insect "cumshot" on her body she will simply eat it, and though human males might find this exciting it doesn't do anything for the more pragmatic and instinctive sensibilities of male insects. Some species of cricket have therefore developed a kind of prostitution transaction: the male gives the female a big bag of food, and while she's busy eating it he attaches his sperm and relies on her being too busy with her dinner to remove the packet until it's already too late. Some of these crickets are the equivalent of deceptive human men who try to pad the envelope with low-denomination bills or slips of paper secreted among the large ones; they gather large quantities of low-nutrition food and hope the females don't notice how cheap they are.

Some species of flies have a similar strategy, though their sex actually involves a form of copulation which takes 5-20 minutes; the longer the act, the higher the chance of proper insemination, so the larger the food donation the longer the female is kept busy eating it and the longer she will let him have her, thus the higher the chance his genes will be passed on. Flies who are "wealthier" (i.e. better at food-gathering) have a better choice of mates, and more generous clients get to buy larger blocks of ladies' time, just as in human society.

Female spiders are generally much larger than males of their species, so their relationship could be viewed as the arachnid equivalent of a client seeking a dominatrix. Unlike many human dominatrices these ladies give full service, but among redback spiders (*Latrodectus hasselti*, cousins of the black widow) the price is so high that this type of session is literally a once-in-a-lifetime experience. Everyone knows that black widows generally kill and eat their mates, but their males at least attempt to escape after the "wedding"; the male redback, on the other hand, is the ultimate masochist of the arthropod world. In order to ensure that his sperm will have time to inseminate the *femme fatale* of his choice, he attaches his packet to her abdomen and then literally dives into her mouth, ensuring that she will be occupied in devouring him until it is far too late to remove the sperm. Talk about paying the ultimate price! Most human men like having *part* of their anatomy in a woman's mouth, but in my humble opinion the redbacks carry this to extremes.

The Pit

We are the Martians now. – Barbara Judd (Barbara Shelley)

One of my favorite horror movies is *Quatermass and the Pit* (1967), released in the United States as *Five Million Years to Earth*. IMDb synopsizes its plot thus: "An ancient Martian spaceship is unearthed in London, and proves to have powerful psychic effects on the people around." If you've seen the movie you already know that doesn't remotely do it justice, and if you haven't (but would like to) you might want to skip this essay for now because it uses the film's plot as a metaphor for human behavior, and that necessarily involves major spoilers. If you've already seen the movie, or don't like science fiction-style horror (or horror-tinged sci-fi), or you just don't mind knowing the end of a flick you might someday watch, stick around. And even if you know it well, please have patience while I describe those plot elements crucial to the comparison.

The synopsis says the ship is "unearthed"; that happens during the excavation of a new Underground station at Hobbs End, a locale long associated with ghostly goings-on. Of course the immediate assumption is that the find is an unexploded bomb left over from the Blitz, but tests quickly prove that the thing has been there for a hell of a lot longer... five million years, give or take. It is also, needless to say, not

The Pit

of this Earth. Further investigation by Professor Quatermass and his associates reveals that its origin is Mars, and it contains the mummified bodies of its crew (who were killed on impact) and several hominids who appear to have been artificially altered. Research and various incidents reveal the full truth: though the Martians knew their world was dying, they could not colonize the Earth because the gravity was too heavy and the air too dense for their fragile, locust-like bodies. They therefore decided to re-engineer the brains of Earth's primitive inhabitants so that they would think and act like Martians; in other words, they would essentially make Martians in human bodies to survive on Earth. But the experiment was only in its early stages when the Martian civilization collapsed; they were never able to reprogram enough members of our race for the experiment to fully succeed. It did, however, introduce certain elements into the human gene pool.

The Martians had what we would call psychic abilities, and though the plan was incomplete it did result in some humans displaying such abilities in latent form... abilities which could be awakened by the artificial psychic presence which served the function of a ship's computer. Over the millennia, sensitive individuals living in the area above the buried ship received signals from it and saw ghostly apparitions of Martians (which they perceived as horned goblins or devils, hence the name of the place). As the movie approaches its climax, an accident re-awakens the ship's damaged consciousness, which immediately sets about fulfilling its original mission: to create a Martian colony out of the area's humans. The Martians, as previously mentioned, were insect-like creatures who lived in tremendous hives; as one might expect of insects, they had little individuality and no tolerance for deviation from the norm. They therefore underwent periodic purges, events in which mass hysteria raced through the hives and caused them to exterminate all whom they sensed were too different to be allowed to live. And they intended us to live the same way, undergoing occasional periods in which those more like our Martian creators – unimaginative, conformist and easily driven by the hive-mind – would gather in mobs to seek out and destroy those who were too different, using the psychic technology at their command. Until he is shaken out of it by the more-purely-human Dr. Roney, even the brilliant Professor Quatermass is swallowed up in the hysteria, unable to use his critical thinking abilities while in the grip of the blind drive to destroy everyone who is different.

Of course, this is all a mere fantasy; we know humans don't carry any hidden bombs in our unconscious minds. We know there aren't any evolutionary relics, behaviors designed to advance some greater biological purpose with a complete disregard for what individuals might want. We know that humans don't behave differently when they're in mobs, and that such mobs don't really engage in horrible acts their members would condemn if they were committed by individuals. We know that people don't allow themselves to be guided by sinister "authorities" about whom they actually know nothing, and that they don't blindly obey laws they had no part in creating. We know that people are never terrified of imaginary devils which exist only in their minds, and that they aren't subject to periods of irrational hysteria in which they discard millennia of moral development in a blind, monstrous quest to purge all Outsiders from society.

Don't we?

Quite Contrary

It is the mark of an educated mind to be able to entertain a thought without accepting it. – Aristotle

I've always been a firm believer in free thought. Even in high school I preferred to talk to someone who disagreed with me because of his own independent thought processes, rather than one who agreed with me because some "authority" had told him mine was the correct position. One day when I was about 19 I was going into the Liberal Arts Building at UNO and had to pass a young man and a young woman who were engaged in a heated argument; I didn't know either of them but apparently they thought I looked "normal" because as I approached I heard the guy say, "OK, we'll ask *her*!" He then turned to me and asked, "Don't you agree that abortion is murder?"

I immediately replied, "Well, I think it's killing, but I also think killing is sometimes justified." They were both dumbstruck, and I kept on going. Their reaction told me everything I needed to know about both of them and their stupid argument; had either of them arrived at his position by logic (or any other kind of independent thought) he wouldn't have been so surprised to hear a complex and unusual answer. But because both of them had obtained their opinions from leaders who had told them what to think, they couldn't understand any answer to that question other than a binary "yes" or "no". They had both bought into a false dichotomy and been issued a checklist of statements with which they had to agree in order to become accepted members of the Young Fascists for the Fatherland or the Kampus Kommies (respectively), and an answer which fit on

177

neither list shut them down like the androids on Mudd's Planet.

I'm not quite as much of an insufferable smartass as I was at 19, but I still respect people who disagree with me, especially when they in turn respect me for disagreeing with them. As I wrote in my essay "Never Too Many",

> I have readers who identify as libertarian, liberal, conservative, socialist, anarchist, minarchist, monarchist and apolitical, and who call themselves Pagans, Christians, Muslims, Jews, Hindus, Buddhists, agnostics and atheists. Some consider themselves feminists, others men's rights advocates, others anti-feminists or humanists or transhumanists or environmentalists or intellectuals or just "geeks"…But the one thing you all have in common is a recognition that it is wrong for government to use brute force to suppress the right of individuals to associate with whomever they choose, however they choose and for whatever reason they choose, even if money is involved.

Sometimes my readers disagree with me, and sometimes y'all disagree with each other, but it's rare that I see name-calling or other ugliness; for the most part my readership is one of the most civil and mutually-respectful groups on the whole internet, and I'm very proud of that. But in a very small number of cases a reader has announced their disagreement not with a "Well, Maggie, I respect you but I think you're wrong on this," or a "We're just going to have to agree to disagree on that," or even a "What the hell were you smoking when you wrote this, you silly tart?" but rather with a stated or implied ultimatum: "If you dare to disagree with me again, I'm going to stop reading you."

Frankly, this sort of thing makes me scratch my head; I'm not sure what such a person really hopes to accomplish. Everyone who's ever written to me knows that I'm very generous with my time and help when approached nicely, but anyone who's ever read more than three of my essays can probably guess how I react to threats; it's the difference between stroking a cat's fur the right way or the wrong way. It's inevitable that once in a while, a regular reader will begin to find that they're disagreeing with me a bit too often to enjoy reading any more, and so stops; there's certainly nothing wrong with that. Life is too short to annoy oneself unnecessarily, and I certainly wouldn't stick around on a blog where I felt uncomfortable or unwelcome. But neither would I make an ass of myself by demanding that a prolific and strong-willed writer change her style or opinions to suit the whims of one reader, and neither should anyone else.

Rooted in Racism

We have only to remember that virility was one of the special features of the savage woman…we have portraits of Red Indian and Negro beauties, whom it is difficult to recognize for women, so huge are their jaws and cheekbones, so hard and coarse their features. – Cesare Lombroso, from an explanation of why whores are subhuman

For most of history, the only people writing about prostitutes were outsiders, mostly men, and as the Christian Era wore on such writings were increasingly based in some kind of moral agenda (with a concomitant bias against whores). After the Reformation the idea of the prostitute as victim first appeared, and by the 19th century had become the dominant theme in "studies" which, though they often pretended to be "scientific" in keeping with the mania of the day, were actually nothing more than Christian anti-whore propaganda dressed up in scientific garb so as to support the dominant view that "normal" women were pure and asexual, and therefore any woman who was sexual had to be some sort of monster. Not that this was her *fault*, mind you; since all women were regarded as childlike simpletons only unenlightened brutes like the police thought of whores as malefactors. "Educated" men and early feminists alike claimed that we were just born that way, rather like atavisms or congenital idiots, and therefore had to be protected from our own decisions and "uplifted" from the condition into which we had "fallen".

Unfortunately for these earnest do-gooders, the vast majority of hookers refused to be "uplifted" into such soul-stirring and rewarding careers as domestic service or factory work, and further studies continued to reveal that though most whores came from the "degraded" lower classes, some came from solid middle-class families and should have "known better". This was of particular concern in the United States, whose prevailing belief-system made the very idea of class unthinkable unless the individual was of one of the "degraded races" (mostly black people, Jews, Italians and Irish). From such racist manure grew early 20th-century views on prostitution; though most prostitutes were merely lazy criminals of questionable ancestry, white girls of predominantly Anglo-Saxon, French or Germanic ancestry *must* have been forced into the trade by evil (usually dark-skinned) "pimps". This doublethink spawned contradictory hysterias: on the one hand there was a mad rush to enact anti-prostitution laws designed to arrest, punish and "correct" prostitutes of low birth and/or dark skin, while at the same time a moral panic arose over middle-class white girls abducted into the "white slave" trade, and a body of laws were enacted to put a halt to this nonexistent social evil.

The First World War gave Europeans something real to worry about, but the panic continued in the United States until the Great Depression served the same function. Fascism soon reared its ugly head, followed by the Cold War, so anti-prostitution hysteria slept peacefully in its grave for decades. Oh, the prohibitionist laws were still in place; police departments continued to persecute and bully women who were trying to make a living, and occasionally a moral reformer might attempt to whip up a pogrom against whores. Or perhaps a maker of exploitation films would attempt to rekindle the "white slave" panic (with drug addiction as a new element in the myth), but for the most part, people weren't all that worried about prostitutes. By the 1960s early second-wave feminists were talking about decriminalization, and positive portrayals of "high end" call girls were becoming more common in movies and television (though poor streetwalkers were still depicted as invariably under the control of evil, and usually black, pimps).

Unfortunately, this upward trend was not to last; the events of the 1960s gave rise to two major reactionary movements which eventually got in bed with one another to plot further violence against sex workers. The anti-sex feminists appeared in the 1970s, gradually took over feminism by cynically manipulating the doctrine of sisterhood, and used anti-sex panic generated by the AIDS epidemic to completely take over mainstream feminism by the mid-'80s. Meanwhile, the changing face of American culture which followed the upheavals of the '60s (including feminism, desegregation, the sexual revolution and computerization) added fuel to the long-smoldering fire of Puritanism, causing a wave of religious fundamentalism to sweep the country in the 1980s. And though feminism and religious fundamentalism might seem bitter enemies to some, their shared hatred of sex (especially sexual freedom for women) drew them inexorably together (*see "Feminists and Other Puritans" in volume II*), and they soon joined forces against porn and all forms of sex work (though apparently agreeing to disagree on abortion). Fundies began to include feminist "degradation" and "victimization" rhetoric in their anti-sex screeds, and found it worked to influence "progressive" lawmakers who viewed arguments based in Christian morality as radioactive. The turn of the century saw the two in a night-shrouded graveyard together, quietly digging up the corpse of "white slavery" and reanimating it to serve their prohibitionist agenda. But just as the zombies so popular in recent horror films can be recognized as the people they once were, so trafficking hysteria's congenital racism is still visible under the gangrene and grave dirt.

Don't expect any of the trafficking fanatics to admit it; in fact many of them take conscious or unconscious steps to hide it. Feminists have converted the racism into sexism, so that rather than being about "inferior races" victimizing helpless WASPs, it's about "oppressive" men victimizing helpless women. And though mainstream trafficking fetishists are careful to insist that "it happens all over the world," it should be obvious to even the most obtuse that trafficking mythology has grown along with prejudice against "illegal aliens", especially those from Latin America, Eastern Europe, Africa and East Asia. "Traffickers" are nearly always cast as ethnic, usually tied to foreign organized crime cartels, and a disproportionate number of those women

Rooted in Racism

"investigated" as "trafficking victims" are themselves foreign. As Laura Agustín has repeatedly written, a great deal of the widespread belief in "trafficking" derives from the racist assumption that people (especially women) from developing countries aren't clever enough or sophisticated enough to plan a migration to a more economically robust country (*see page 145*), to seek out those who can assist them in circumventing measures designed to keep them out, and to decide on a means of work which supports them while keeping them below the radar of immigration authorities.

Because overt racism is uncomfortable to many modern people, the desire to keep foreigners out is often cloaked in paternalistic concern for their welfare. But because of the admixture of feminism with the "white slavery" mythology, men who cross borders in an unorthodox fashion are generally represented as lawbreaking "illegal aliens" or "human traffickers", while women are more often cast as passive victims (hence the repeated claims that the vast majority of "trafficked persons" are women and children). Laws based in this dogma often prosecute the husbands or boyfriends of sex workers as "pimps" or "human traffickers", and dismiss any denial from the woman as the product of "brainwashing"; in other cases, laws designed ostensibly to "protect victims of trafficking" are worded in such a way as to "rescue" underage white prostitutes while criminalizing underage nonwhite ones. But in every case, anti-trafficking laws are really about separating people into two groups (whether by race, by sex or by national origin), and denying them *both* freedom by casting the one as competent (and therefore liable to criminal charges) and the other as incompetent (and therefore in need of "rescue" for their own good). The distinctions allow governments and their supporters to pretend they exercise some form of objective moral discernment, but they are ultimately immaterial to the whore; whether she is incarcerated, institutionalized or deported, she is not allowed to live her life in peace, and whether she is criminalized, demonized or infantilized her judgment and right to adult agency are entirely disregarded.

Tales from the Dark Side

An inability to tell fantasy from reality would normally be considered evidence of psychosis, but in law enforcement it's a job requirement. – Maggie McNeill

Since at least the time of Plato, the natural world was generally viewed in Western thought as corrupt, foul and bad; this idea entered Christianity via Gnosticism and dominated philosophy until the advent of the Romantic Era in the late 18th century. Anything of the natural world (including, of course, sex) was to be looked down upon and avoided whenever possible; the things of the mind and spirit were what was important, and those who wished to appear superior to others removed themselves from the natural world and eschewed the "pleasures of the flesh" (at least in public). The Romantics, however, rejected all that; they taught that the natural world was innately good, that childhood "innocence" (i.e. closeness to the natural state) was a thing to be cherished, that primitive people were "noble savages", and that "natural" living was purer and better than "artificial". This was decidedly a minority viewpoint; the growing middle

class of 19th-century Europe and America still saw untamed
Nature as rather nasty, and those who lived closer to it than
they (in other words, the working class) as inferiors to be
"improved" by curing them of their dedication to physical
pleasures such as sex and liquor.

But humans are not known for logical consistency,
and the *bourgeois* less so than most; as the Victorian Era
wore on, some elements of Romantic philosophy were
absorbed into the common *weltanschauung*, even when they
contradicted other aspects of it. For example, the
"innocence" of children became the center of a veritable cult
despite the fact that adults were expected to behave in an
incredibly artificial manner, and "natural" foods and
medicines were all the rage in the "social purity" crowd
because they were believed to excite the (natural) physical
passions less than highly processed ones! But if the
Victorians' beliefs were incongruous, those of the neo-
Victorians are even worse: while they reject the belief that
sex is innately bad, they also believe against all reason and
evidence that it's something like a radioactive material which
must be handled with special and elaborate precautions or
else it becomes the single most destructive force on Earth.
They imagine that engaging in sex for the "wrong" reasons,
or without the benediction of elaborate rituals of consent, or
with people separated from one another by more than a very
few years of age, is terribly harmful. They believe that
merely taking pictures of the taboo act creates a kind of
Gorgonic icon which drives its viewers mad, and that the
mere *existence* of such images harms women and children
who are not even in close proximity to them. And they
fervently assert that it is so incredibly dangerous to the sacred

"innocence" of "children" (a term which refers not to true children, but to a ritual category which actually includes some adults), for anyone to even *imagine* sexual contact with them, that those who indulge in these Forbidden Thoughts deserve penalties greater than those for violent assault, followed by lifelong social ostracism.

Needless to say, most of this has only the most tenuous basis in reality, and some of it none at all. But the desire to describe Nature (especially sex) as "good" or "bad" is a very strong one, and for the neo-Victorian mind to accept sex into the "good" category it must be ritually purified by amputating all of its darker aspects, branding even the *discussion* of them as "violence", and even pretending that they aren't even sex at all (*see page 62*). This belief flies in the face of reality; sex, fear, dominance and violence are inextricably bound together (*see "Eros and Phobos" in volume II*), and only by living in a state of complete denial can someone pretend that the only valid, "healthy" and *legal* sex is that which is so sanitized and neutered that it resembles the real thing about as closely as a hamburger does a heifer. Even many unadventurous people have a few rather dark fantasies or repressed turn-ons, and a few have fantasies that if acted upon would be evil indeed (as my friend Philippa used to say, "good fantasy, bad reality"). But the mere existence of violent, dark fantasies does not indicate a corresponding plan to carry them out; probably 99% of all sexual fantasies are never acted upon, and when it comes to those involving unquestionably evil acts I'm sure the percentage is higher still. Furthermore, the mere discussion of such fantasies with others does not constitute a conspiracy to turn them into reality. But in a world where prosecution for thoughtcrime has become a grim reality, it might be wise to restrict such discussions to fully-anonymized online

186

accounts and to encrypt any files referring to the fantasy; otherwise you could end up like Gilberto Valle:

> …agents with the Federal Bureau of Investigation took Officer Valle into custody…after they uncovered several plots to kidnap, rape, cook and eat women…the officer's estranged wife recently contacted the F.B.I. to report that…[he] viewed and kept disturbing items on his computer…[though he] never followed through on any of the acts he is accused of discussing. His lawyer…said the officer committed no crime. "At worst, this is someone who has sexual fantasies…There is no actual crossing the line from fantasy to reality," she added…(*NY Times*, 10/26/12)

At first I leaned toward believing the allegations, but the more I thought about it the more I realized that these were almost certainly no more than extreme fantasies used by a vindictive ex to put him away; the only reason I had given the story as much credence as I did was that it's very easy to believe a cop capable of acts of extreme, non-consensual sadism. Then just a few months later, I went from "almost certain" to "dead certain":

> A high-ranking police official…and a former high-school librarian were charged…in a plot to kidnap, torture and kill women and children, federal prosecutors said. Richard Meltz…and Robert Christopher Asch…were held without bail…Peter Brill, an attorney for Mr. Meltz, said his client "had no interest or intention of hurting anybody…it was never anything other than a fantasy"…An official said the case against the men grew out of an investigation in which a …New York Police Department officer was charged and convicted in a plot to kidnap, rape, cook and eat women.

The...officer, Gilberto Valle, was convicted in March and is awaiting sentencing (*Wall Street Journal*, 4/16/13).

Valle's conviction was later overturned on appeal. I don't know about you, but I've never heard of an organized interstate gang of serial killers who plot capers for months on the internet without ever carrying a single one out. I think it's pretty obvious that what the defense attorneys in both cases said is true: these are men with a very extreme BDSM fantasy who are being sacrificed to further the dominant cultural myth that sex can be purified, sanctified and tamed.

Universal Criminality

Find out just what any people will quietly submit to and you have found out the exact measure of injustice and wrong which will be imposed upon them.
– Frederick Douglass

For years I've warned that the United States was moving toward a state I call "universal criminality"; as I explained in "Creating Criminals" (*see page 5*), governments of the late 19th and early 20th centuries realized that the easiest and most subtle means of social control is simply to establish so many complex, broad, vague, intrusive and mutually contradictory laws that every single person is in violation of at least some of them at any given time. Then when any "authority" from the chief executive down to the lowliest cop wants to teach one of the peons a lesson, all he has to do is find a law to charge him with and the machine then proceeds to grind him up psychologically, financially, politically and often physically.

188

Universal Criminality

The process began with the "social purity" laws which criminalized behaviors (such as drinking, prostitution or even masturbation) which were previously considered private. It then grew during the Great Depression, proliferated in the post-World War II era (mostly under the excuse of "security"), and increased exponentially after the mid-1980s, at which point I began to see the writing on the wall. There are now so many criminal laws that they are literally uncountable; the last serious attempt to enumerate them was made in 1982, and that failed miserably. The Department of Justice estimates that there are over 4500 federal "crimes" and over 300,000 regulations with felony-level criminal penalties, and that grows by over 50 new "crimes" and innumerable regulations every year. And that's only *federal* crimes; multiply that number by some other x factor (10-40 perhaps?) to estimate the number of state laws, and roughly 40,000 new state laws go into effect every year. Then there are county and municipal laws...

Obviously it's impossible for anyone to know all of these, but "ignorance of the law is no excuse" (except for cops); the requirement for the prosecution to prove *mens rea* (criminal intent) was discarded sometime in the '90s, and juries are routinely (and incorrectly) instructed that if the prosecution can prove the facts they must vote to convict even if they believe the defendant did not intend to do anything wrong. Of course, that only applies to citizens; government actors, including cops, prosecutors and even judges, are excused as "acting in good faith" even when a defense attorney can prove that a victim has been charged with something that isn't a crime, or when the cop or prosecutor actively breaks laws himself in order to persecute

189

a victim. Given all these facts, no one can declare with certainty when the goal of universal criminality in the United States was reached, but it's probable that it happened sometime early in this century when politicians again used the excuse of "security" to gut the Bill of Rights, shred the last intact portions of the Constitution, and establish procedures which enshrined police and other government actors as *de facto* nobles, a ruling class who are subject to neither laws nor common human decency.

Cops are now allowed to arrest anyone for any reason (including "suspicion"); invade the homes of citizens without cause or warrant; maim or murder them (and their children and pets) without consequence; steal their property (and keep it even if the victim is never charged with a crime); and brutalize, rob and arrest anyone who tries to document the behavior. Citizen complaints are either ignored or handled with token "investigations" by the same department which is accused of the crimes; these "investigations" invariably result in exoneration of the criminal "officers" or infliction of penalties so minor they constitute a further insult to the victims. Prosecutors can charge one action or group of actions with any of *dozens* of charges, and will generally reserve several so if the first trial goes against them, they can use the others to get a new trial for the same offense without violating prohibitions against double jeopardy; even with no reasonable grounds for prosecution they can often continue the process indefinitely until they either "win" or bankrupt and ruin the defendant. They routinely lie, threaten and withhold exculpatory evidence, because the SCOTUS has granted them absolute immunity from either criminal or civil charges for their actions. And most judges are either tyrants who ignore the law to enforce their own whims, or bored bureaucrats who let cops and prosecutors get away with whatever they like. However, if any of these employees of the "justice system" commits a crime, it will be swept under the rug, excused completely or "punished" with a sentence several orders of magnitude less than that with which a private citizen would be inflicted.

Want to know what it's like to live in a police state? Look around you. Like the legendary frog, Americans have remained content to sit in the pot while the temperature has gradually increased, and we're all well and truly cooking now. The last of our civil liberties are being stripped away at a frightening rate, Congress is moving to take control of the internet, and legislation enacted near the end of Obama's first term gave the president power to use the military to indefinitely detain U.S. citizens without charge or trial (on "suspicion of terrorism") if they own guns, are missing fingers or have more than 7 days' worth of food in their houses. The government no longer even pretends to answer to the people: half of all Americans now recognize it as "an immediate threat to the rights and freedoms of ordinary citizens", only 5% of Americans believe that Congress is doing a decent job, and in January of 2012 a White House spokesman declared the majority of Americans who support marijuana legalization to be "extremists". If you haven't yet read Václav Havel's "The Power of the Powerless" (available as a download on my blog's Resources page), now might be a good time to do so.

Whorearchy

I have no respect for the passion for equality, which seems to me merely idealizing envy.
– Oliver Wendell Holmes Jr

Among the few facts about sex work that everyone agrees upon is that there is a "whorearchy", a sort of class system among sex workers. Now, nobody agrees on anything *about* that system, only that it exists. Many porn performers, strippers, dominatrices, etc insist not only that they aren't whores, but that they're *better* than we are; those whose professions have separated enough from ours that they aren't even considered sex workers any more (such as actresses and *especially* masseuses) can be very pompous about it (*see "Drawing Lines" in volume II*). Prostitutes, on the other hand, sometimes see themselves as better, smarter, more discreet, etc than strippers or porn performers; sugar babies and other halfway whores deny that they're sex workers at all; and some unusually self-deluded escorts will even try to draw imaginary lines separating themselves from other hookers. "Authorities" in criminalization and legalization regimes devote great effort to erecting arbitrary barriers between "tolerable" and "intolerable" varieties of harlotry, and sometimes to cementing the strata in place; cops and prosecutors delight in tricking "legal" sex workers into breaking their ridiculous rules (or falsely claiming that they did) in order to have an excuse for victimizing them; and sex worker advocates expend considerable efforts in hand-wringing and lamentation over "classism".

To a degree, these activists are right; a whore is a whore is a whore, and legal, moral or procedural lines serve

192

Whorearchy

only to break people into smaller groups which are more easily dominated by the power-hungry. If you accept money from someone that he gives due to sexual interest in you, then you are a whore and everything else is just semantics. When politicians, pundits or rulers use some arbitrary determinant like penetration, duration, location or motivation to bless some harlots while damning others, what they're actually doing is reducing the size of the group who might oppose them and winning supporters from among those granted legitimacy. This is why I'm harshly unsympathetic to those who vehemently maintain that their species of sex work or sensual therapy is absolutely *not* sex work: all they're doing is throwing other women under the bus, and if we had all stuck together from the beginning of second-wave feminism half a century ago, prostitution would've been decriminalized long ago and many women who are now dead or damaged might still be alive and healthy.

At the same time, it's madness to pretend that at the present level of human evolution there can ever be such a thing as a classless society. Human beings, like other social animals, naturally form cliques, packs and tribes, and such groups inevitably develop hierarchies. Some people are natural leaders and others natural followers, even outside of a formal structure; the Founding Fathers intended the US to be classless, but look what's happened to it. Nor are Marxists (and hipsters playing at Marxism) correct in their insistence that it's always the rich who control everything; at our present stage of history money is indeed the single most powerful force, but it hasn't always been that way and won't always be in the future. And those who rail about "the 1%" forget that there are lots of ways to get into that fraction:

birth, popularity, talent, intelligence, ambition, luck, sex appeal, and even plain animal cunning are all paths to riches and power, so pretending that there is still some elite caste inevitably born to the purple is disingenuous in the extreme. Even those who are uninterested in influence over others sometimes find themselves in a position of leadership or control; some people have superior organizational skills, determination or intelligence which allows them to build infrastructures in which others freely choose to participate in exchange for money or whatever other return the organizer needs. Such a person may suddenly find themselves the "boss" of a company, co-op or club whom others turn to for guidance, even though the only motivation at the start was to make things easier, better or more comfortable for themselves and their immediate dependents.

This is why I tend to tune out when people start blathering about "privilege" as though it were some specific quality like height, skin color, IQ or income. There is no single quality in the modern world which confers "privilege" as birth once could, not even money or education. Certainly some people are underprivileged and others start out with greater advantages, but this is inevitable in a world where everyone is different; even the *word* "privilege" plays into an authoritarian paradigm where there are no natural, inalienable rights, only "privileges" granted by beneficent "leaders" (*see page 81*). Furthermore, early advantages no more ensure success than early disadvantages guarantee failure, and in fact a growing number of psychologists point out that too much privilege often makes a child (and the adult he becomes) fragile, maladjusted and less likely to succeed than one who has to struggle to achieve his goals. It is as pointless to feel guilty about one's natural advantages as it is to resent those with other advantages one lacks.

Whorearchy

What it all boils down to is this: people are drawn to different kinds of work and have different aptitudes and comfort levels. Some women like one kind of sex work, some another; some prefer doing lots of low-dollar calls and others a few high-dollar ones. Some fall into management roles without trying, while others avoid such roles at all costs. Many if not most sex workers drift or migrate from one kind of work to another, or in and out of sex work entirely, as their circumstances and needs change; someone who was safely "legal" yesterday may be "illegal" tomorrow. This is why it is absolutely imperative that we not allow troublemakers from either inside or outside of the *demimonde* to divide us by drawing lines in the sand and turning those on one side of the line against those on the other. We need to stop obsessing about the whorearchy and pretending it can or should be eradicated, but we also need to oppose those who wish to calcify it in order to employ it as a tool of control.

Storyville

All you old-time queens, from New Orleans/
Who lived in Storyville
You sang the blues, try to amuse/
Here's how they pay the bill
The law step in and call it sin to have a little fun
The police car has made a stop and Storyville is done. –
Clarence Williams, "Farewell To Storyville"

195

The Essential Maggie McNeill

New Orleans was founded on May 7, 1718 by Jean-Baptiste Le Moyne de Bienville, and named for Philippe, Duke of Orléans, who was Regent of France at the time. Besides being terribly primitive like all new colonies, New Orleans was hot, mosquito-infested and disease-ridden and therefore had nothing to recommend it to women, so Bienville petitioned King Louis XV for help in 1721. The monarch responded by releasing all the prostitutes in La Salpêtrière prison and deporting them to New Orleans, where they of course resumed their trade. So many of the early female inhabitants of the city were whores that when a priest suggested to one of the first governors of Louisiana that he banish all "disreputable women", the governor replied, "If I send away all the loose females, there will be no women left here at all." In 1728, the Ursuline nuns started to import convent-raised middle-class French girls as wives for the middle and upper-class male colonists and continued to do so until 1751; these were called "casket girls" (*filles à la cassette*) because the French government issued them small chests of clothing.

Most of the female population were still either whores or former whores, but this concerned few people other than the priests; prostitution in New Orleans was neither regulated nor suppressed at any time during the 18th century. The colony was ceded to Spain by the Treaty of Paris (1763) and remained Spanish territory until 1801, when Napoleon reclaimed it, then sold it to the United States in the Louisiana Purchase of 1803. Obviously, the puritanical Americans could not allow things to stand as they were, so though prostitution was still legal a series of regulations were imposed to allow the police to arrest streetwalkers for "vagrancy" or harass madams for "brothel keeping". Most of these cases were dropped long before trial because the men

196

who owned brothels or rented rooms to streetwalkers wanted their tenants back at work, and paid bribes or hired lawyers to ensure that outcome. New Orleans' first actual prostitution law was the 1857 Lorette ordinance which banned brothels on the first floor of buildings; it was soon declared unconstitutional, but the advent of the American Civil War gave the city fathers more important things to worry about.

New Orleans was captured by the Union Navy in May of 1862 and placed under martial law with General Benjamin Butler in command; he was known as "Beast Butler" for his tyrannical orders and "Spoons Butler" for his habit of stealing the silverware of every house he stayed in during the war. Butler seized $800,000 from the Dutch consulate, jailed French and English citizens (including diplomats), arrested clergymen for refusing to pray for President Lincoln, and within days of occupying the city issued his infamous General Order #28, which stated that if any woman should "...show contempt for any officer or soldier of the United States, she shall be regarded and shall be held liable to be treated as a woman of the town plying her avocation", in other words a prostitute. This order provoked widespread outcry even in the North and was officially protested by both England and France; it was almost certainly the cause of Butler's dismissal from the post only seven months later.

After Butler's removal the working-class whores of New Orleans thrived on the business generated by lonely soldiers far from home, and by the end of the war a whole string of brothels had opened along the old Basin Canal; the road which connected them was named Basin Street after the canal, and the brothels there and all over the city continued to thrive during the Reconstruction on the money brought in by the Carpetbaggers, unscrupulous Northern businessmen who flocked to the South to take advantage of its weakened economic condition. Most of these merchants built their mansions along Nyades Road to the nearby town of Carrolton; the road was renamed St. Charles Avenue and the railway which ran along it was eventually converted to a streetcar line which is still used today.

By 1897 there were brothels all over the city, so Alderman Sidney Story proposed to limit the trade to one district specifically zoned for the purpose. The district chosen was the Basin Street area where most of the larger and better bordellos had grown up during the Occupation and Reconstruction; specifically, it was the zone bounded by Iberville, Basin, St. Louis, and N. Robertson streets. Residents simply referred to the area as "The District"; only contemporary newspapers and later historians called it "Storyville" after the official who had proposed it. The brothels ranged from 50¢ "cribs" (originally a San Francisco term) to mid-range houses charging $1-$5, up to a row of elegant mansions along Basin Street where the girls charged $10, a great deal of money in a day when the average workman earned 22¢/hour. The most expensive fee was probably that charged by Madame Kate Townsend, who though she had long retired from active whoring would still agree to see an important client if he was willing to pay her exorbitant fee of $50/hour!

A catalog named *The Blue Book* was published periodically by the wealthier brothels; its title page was inscribed with the motto of the Order of the Garter (*honi soit qui mal y pense*, "shame to him who evil thinks") and its interior contained descriptions of each house and its featured girls, a price list and a description of any special services offered. The most lavish of the mansions was probably the

Storyville

Arlington (named for its owner, Josie Arlington) at 225 Basin Street, described in *The Blue Book* as "absolutely and unquestionably the most decorative and costly fitted-out sporting palace ever placed before the American public." The Arlington was a four-story edifice with a distinctive onion-domed cupola, crammed with expensive paintings and statuary and featuring various parlors decorated in the styles of foreign countries. Josie Arlington herself was a remarkably ethical woman; in a day when verifiable virgin whores brought a whopping $200 or more and previously-wealthy Creole families who had fallen on hard times often sent their beautiful, cultured daughters to the best brothels, she absolutely refused to allow virgins to be "defiled or exploited" by her business. In fact, the tomb in which she was originally buried (though her body was later moved to foil curiosity-seekers and the structure was sold to the Morales family) features a bronze figure of a young girl who is thought to symbolize a virgin being turned away from the door of the Arlington.

Black, white and Creole brothels (the latter staffed by beautiful "quadroon" or "octoroon" girls, $\frac{1}{4}$ or $\frac{1}{8}$ black respectively) coexisted in Storyville, but these were all for white clients; black men were legally barred from hiring any girl in the District. However, brothels where black girls accepted black clients were tolerated in a separate district nearby; they were technically illegal but neither the police nor the regulators ever harassed them. And though jazz did not originate in Storyville as is commonly believed, it was played by musicians in the more expensive houses and was therefore first heard in Storyville by many out-of-town clients, becoming inextricably associated with it in those gentlemen's minds. "Jelly Roll" Morton and "Pops" Foster started out as musicians in Storyville brothels, and Louis Armstrong's mother worked in one of the houses after she was abandoned by his father.

Considering its success and the amount of revenue it brought to the city, Storyville might still exist today if not for the prudery of Secretary of the Navy Josephus Daniels, a teetotaler who considered the district as a "bad influence" on the sailors at the nearby Naval base during World War I. The District was therefore closed by federal order in 1917 over the strong objections of the New Orleans city government and Mayor Martin Behrman, who said "You can make prostitution illegal, but you can't make it unpopular." The closing of the District is dramatized in a scene from the movie *New Orleans* (1947), in which Billie Holiday and Louis Armstrong perform the haunting "Farewell to Storyville"; though most of the working girls were forcibly evicted, new brothels opened in secret both there and in other parts of the city, streetwalkers proliferated and some of the earliest call girls appeared. Many of the old houses were converted into dance halls, cabarets and restaurants, and after the beginning of Prohibition many speakeasies and gambling dens joined the clandestine brothels. Frequent police and federal raids failed to hinder operations, so in the early 1930s the city government (at federal urging) bought or seized most of the area and leveled every building (even the beautiful mansions on Basin Street) to make room for the squalid Iberville Housing Project, which remained until it was shut down after Hurricane Katrina (archeologists were allowed to study the area after the project was torn down, and made some interesting Storyville discoveries). Basin Street was even renamed "North Saratoga", though the original name was restored by popular demand in the 1950s.

Storyville

Sadly, the current political establishment in New Orleans prefers to pretend that Storyville never existed; even an historical marker at the site mentions several jazz musicians who were "on the scene here", but glosses over the industry which employed them with the vague and inaccurate phrase "legalized red light district" (since prostitution was not illegal there before, it could not be "legalized"). Though New Orleans cannot contravene state law, city government is allowed to determine police department policy and could certainly order that sex work is to be tolerated; instead they play sleazy games, harass the strip clubs on Bourbon Street (itself a pale remnant of the once-thriving District) in a foolish and futile attempt to "Disnify" New Orleans, and thereby dishonor the memory of thousands of women who helped build the city.

Honolulu Harlots

Prostitution is one of the oldest vices of the human race, and civilized communities have been experimenting with its control for centuries. The only definite conclusion that has been reached is that it is likely to exist as long as the passions of the human beings remain what they are today. – Victor Houston, in his report to Congress on prostitution in Honolulu

Though the early 20th century social purity crusade came to Hawaii as to every place there were Americans, the anti-whore laws it spawned were never strictly enforced. This is partly due to the fact that neither the natives nor the sizable Asian minority saw prostitution as a "social evil" as the puritanical whites did, and the wealthy planters at the top of white society wanted hookers available to protect their daughters from rape or seduction by laborers or American sailors. As in many other places and times, the police were given the power to "regulate" prostitution in Honolulu, and they did so by establishing a series of practices so Draconian they eventually led to the collapse of the system.

Only brothel work was allowed; independent whoring of any kind was strictly suppressed, and of course madams had no objection because that meant all girls had to work for them (just as in modern Nevada). Every passenger ship was met by the vice squad, and any unescorted woman was assumed to be a prostitute; she was fingerprinted, registered and given a copy of the "Ten Commandments" she was obliged to obey:

She may not visit Waikiki Beach or any other beach except Kailua Beach [across the mountains from Honolulu].
She may not patronize any bars or better class cafes.
She may not own property or an automobile.
She may not have a steady "boyfriend" or be seen on the streets with any men.
She may not marry service personnel.
She may not attend dances or visit golf courses.
She may not ride in the front seat of a taxicab, or with a man in the back seat.
She may not wire money to the mainland without permission of the madam.
She may not telephone the mainland without permission of the madam.
She may not change from one house to another. She may not be out of the brothel after 10:30 at night.

Honolulu Harlots

The police enforced these rules by beatings and threatened eviction from the islands. Though working in Honolulu was lucrative ($30,000 or more per year at a time most women were lucky to make $2000), most girls could only handle it for about six months, and when they left the islands they were not permitted to return for at least a year. Originally most brothels (or "boogie houses" as they were called locally) were in the Iwilei district, but they were later forced to relocate to Hotel Street and a few adjoining parts of Chinatown. They were a normal and accepted part of Hawaiian life; there was no stigma attached to men who patronized them, and most wives even accepted their husbands' going there for the rational reasons I've discussed many times. When Naval ships came in, the lines at the brothels literally stretched down the block, and contemporary accounts describe Honolulu housewives passing unconcernedly through the lines to reach the businesses beyond them. The going rate was $2.00 (a full day's wages) for locals and $3.00 for servicemen; most businesses had two separate doors and waiting areas because, due to pervasive racist attitudes of the time, white sailors did not like to think they were being served by the same girls who attended to the Asian locals. During the Second World War, the demand from servicemen grew so large that most of the better brothels on Hotel Street simply stopped seeing local men altogether. To speed things along, a "bull pen" system was instituted: Hawaiian matrons guarded the doors, turning away any man who was drunk or looked like a troublemaker. Each then paid his fee and received a poker chip, then waited for an available room where he undressed and waited for the whore who was working in the next room; she would come in, collect her chip, inspect him for signs of venereal disease, quickly wash him and do her work. He had three minutes to achieve release, after which she said "aloha" and was off to the next room while he washed up and got dressed. Most brothels required girls to see at least 100 men a day and to work at least 20 days per month, but despite this enormous volume there were only about 166 cases of sexually transmitted disease per year in the entire prostitute population (a number some clueless historians have called "extremely high" when it in fact represents an infinitesimal percentage of the tremendous number of clients).

The "bull pen" system is said to have been the brainchild of Jean O'Hara, a gutsy Irish Catholic native of Chicago. After the attack on Pearl Harbor in December of 1941, many prostitutes fled back to the mainland and many others volunteered to nurse wounded men, lowering the available supply just as the demand increased; O'Hara and many of the other girls used the situation to leverage better working conditions for themselves. First they raised the price to $5.00, but Major Frank Steer, the Army officer in charge of vice under martial law, vetoed that and enforced the $3.00 price. They then began to flout the old rules, going out in public as they wished and enjoying their earnings for the first time. The police chief, William Gabrielson, was furious; how dare these dirty whores flout his regime and pretend to be real people! He complained to General Emmons, the military governor, who told him he didn't care *what* the hookers did as long as they were happy, because happy whores meant happy troops. But Gabrielson couldn't stand his little dictatorship being threatened, so he ordered his men to continue business as usual (and more brutally). In April, 1942 they evicted four prostitutes from a house in Waikiki, and the women complained to Captain Benson of

the military police. Benson told them the civilian police
didn't run things any more, and they could do as they liked;
when Gabrielson heard this he was livid and announced to
the *Honolulu Star-Bulletin* that he was officially turning
control of vice over to the military. Emmons was of course
forced by Washington to deny this, and officially returned
control to Gabrielson while at the same time ordering the
MPs to protect the prostitutes from Gabrielson's uniformed
hooligans.

O'Hara, realizing the tenuousness of the whores'
position, instigated a strike which endured for three weeks in
July of 1942, demanding the basic human rights of American
citizens. The prostitutes pointed out that their work was vital
to the war effort, and they had already collectively purchased
$132,000 in war bonds. The establishment was humiliated
and the newspapers were ordered not to print a word about
the strike, but obviously something had to be done; General
Emmons, in a Solomonic maneuver, made a very calm and
diplomatic appeal to Gabrielson to rescind the movement and
residence restrictions, in return for which the military agreed
to take over the weekly health and hygiene inspections.
Gabrielson had little choice but to comply, and the whores
were afterward free to move about the island as they pleased.
O'Hara took advantage of this to carry out a real estate scam;
she would buy a house in a genteel neighborhood and then let
it be known what she did for a living, at which point she
would be promptly bought out at a considerable profit by
bluenosed neighbors.

Eventually, however, she pushed too hard; in 1944
she published a popular book entitled *My Life As a Honolulu
Prostitute* (later republished as *Honolulu Harlot*). Since the

205

Japanese were in retreat and the islands no longer in danger, martial law had been lifted and a new ruling elite decided that Hawaii would never win statehood if most Americans thought of them as backward "natives"; O'Hara's book called unwelcome attention to an institution now regarded as an embarrassment, and a "concerned citizens" group published a map showing the addresses of every registered prostitute in Honolulu so as to provoke a witch-hunt. The police forcibly evicted prostitutes from their homes and returned them to the brothels, and territorial governor Ingram Stainback sent letters to all the high military officials informing them that prostitution was illegal and asking if they approved of the regulated brothel system. Obviously they could not admit that openly, and so stood by while the police closed the brothels on September 22nd, 1944 and forcibly evicted all of the whores from the islands (or harassed them until they either left or managed to evade police surveillance).

Apparently, Chief Gabrielson soon missed the "good old days" of bullying hookers, because he eventually retired from his position to serve as a "consultant" to the Tokyo police department in catering to U.S. military demands for increased control of prostitutes during the American occupation. Meanwhile, Hawaiian politicians tried to make up for lost time by officially granting cops the "right" to rape sex workers by spelling the permission out in the text of the new prostitution law. When a legislator discovered this provision in 2015 and rewrote the law to scrap it, the cops demanded that their decades-old *droit du seigneur* remain in place, and it probably would've had not the media gotten hold of the story and a public outcry not ensued. Now there's a movement to decriminalize sex work there, which might at last free Hawaiian whores from the tender mercies of cops.

Cleansing Fire

I personally call the type of government which can be removed without violence "democracy", and the other, "tyranny". – Karl Popper

The casual reader can be forgiven for arriving at the erroneous conclusion that I become dreadfully morbid in autumn. It starts subtly as the days grow shorter, increases through October with a number of horror-themed columns, reaches a peak with my annual thanatopsis every Day of the Dead (*see page 92*), then descends into blood and fire four days later when, on Guy Fawkes Day, I always *"call for a rededication of the holiday from a time to burn rebels in effigy to a time to burn tyrants in effigy instead"*:

> Governments need to be reminded (at least annually if not constantly) that they only hold power by the sufferance of *all* the people, not merely the majority, and that the overthrow of any government by a disgruntled minority is always a possibility. I would like to see most if not all politicians and their minions paying for their power and privilege by being forced to live in a constant state of nervous anxiety; maybe then fewer would choose that path and more would concern themselves with keeping all the citizenry happy rather than merely pleasing barely enough of the population to keep themselves in office.

But those who think of all this as morbid are those who narrowly see death as the end of all that is good; I embrace a more pagan view which recognizes that all things must end, that life depends upon the deaths of other organisms, and that old, decaying things must be cleared

207

away – sometimes forcibly – in order to make way for new, younger and often better things. Old people must pass on to make room for new children; dilapidated buildings must be demolished to pave the way for new construction. And old, moribund governments which serve only the entrenched and wealthy must be removed if we are to build new ones which better serve *all* of the people and protect minorities from oppression by both majorities and other, more politically powerful minorities.

When one organism consumes another, the components of the devoured (proteins, fats, carbohydrates, etc) become part of the devourer; when an old building is torn down, sometimes a portion of it (such as the slab, hearth or even sections of walls) may become part of whatever is built on its site. And when a government is replaced, those elements of the old one which worked well are often retained in the new one (as English common law became the basis of American law). At other times, however, the old thing is of no use at all; inedible plants are plowed under to ready a field for farming, and dynamite and bulldozers remove a condemned building. And old governments…well, it's certainly *preferable* to dismantle them peacefully, but those currently in power and those who profit by the *status quo* rarely allow that, and at such times more robust methods may become necessary.

Though some of us have been trying to call attention to the rot at the heart of the Western establishment for years now, we have largely been "voices crying out in the wilderness"; most people prefer to blame some bogeyman such as "capitalism", "patriarchy" or "liberals", or to pretend major issues are mere cosmetic blemishes on an otherwise-hale body politic, or even to deny that there are any problems at all. Meanwhile the rulers, rather than admitting the

Cleansing Fire

systemic problems, prefer to treat government as a colossal game of hot potato, eternally passing the ball forward in the hopes that it will be in someone else's hands when the music at last stops as it inevitably must. But as the events of the last few years have amply demonstrated, the piper is growing steadily more exhausted, and will soon demand his due. Soon we will be forced to change the way we've done things for the past century, whether we like it or not, and the actions of the ruling class (especially that of the US and UK) over the past few decades bode ill for that change being a peaceful one. I think it's safe to predict that there will be fireworks, and not of the pleasant kind. But though fire may be fearsome and horrible, it is part of the natural order of things, and supremely efficient for cleansing decay and purifying the site of a plague. And when the flames die down, as they always do, the ash left behind provides fertile soil for new (and gods willing, healthier) growth.

210

About the Author

Maggie McNeill was a librarian in suburban New Orleans, but after an acrimonious divorce she took up sex work; from 1997 to 2006 she worked first as a stripper, then as a call girl and madam. She eventually married her favorite client and retired to a ranch in Oklahoma, but returned to escorting part-time in 2010 and full-time in 2015 after another divorce (this time amicable) and a move to Seattle. She's been a sex worker rights activist since 2004, and since 2010 has written "The Honest Courtesan" (http://maggiemcneill.wordpress.com/), a daily blog which discusses sex work, politics, anarchism, philosophy and other topics. She has also published articles in venues such as *Reason* and the *Washington Post*; given innumerable lectures, talks, radio & video interviews; and is frequently consulted by academics and journalists as an expert on sex work.

Made in the USA
Middletown, DE
21 January 2020